HOW NEAR A TO ACHIEVING GOALS?

Are you getting bogged down in small details while big chances pass you by?

Are you a slave to a cluttered desk?

Have the pressures of time blurred your perspective?

This is much more than a book on managing your time—it is a book on managing yourself!

It is for the harried but stouthearted . . . for the burdened but determined . . . for the overextended Christian who cares enough about his situation to change it.

Practical and realistic, MANAGING YOUR TIME will show you the way to a richer, more relaxed and fulfilling life.

MANAGING YOUR TIME

Practical Guidelines on the Effective Use of Time

TED W. ENGSTROM

and

R. ALEC MACKENZIE

Foreword by HERBERT J. TAYLOR

President, Club Aluminum Products

ZONDERVAN
PUBLISHING HOUSE
OF THE ZONDERVAN CORPORATION | GRAND RAPIDS. MICHIGAN 49506

ZONDERVAN BOOKS are published by Zondervan Publishing House, 1415 Lake Drive, S.E., Grand Rapids, Michigan 49506, U.S.A.

Printed in the United States of America

FOREWORD

You cannot proceed very far in the reading of this book until you realize that it not only tells you how to manage your time more efficiently but it also covers in a very thorough manner the principles of overall management in the fields of business, education and in the Lord's work.

I have known the authors of this book for many years by character, talent and experience in both the field of business and in numerous successful Christian projects. The authors are particularly well qualified to prepare this most helpful book in the field of management.

The book covers various fields of endeavor and contains excellent Bible quotations as well as quotations from a number of past and present national and international leaders such as Robert Burns, Ralph Waldo Emerson, Dwight D. Eisenhower and Senator Mark Hatfield. One of the best pieces of advice given in this book is that we are trustees of our time and should look to God, the Holy Spirit and the Bible for guidance as to how we should use our time and talents.

We all realize the importance of objectives in our lives. If you know what a person's objective is or what is causing him to move in a certain direction, then you are better qualified to advise or to influence him. This book places the proper emphasis on the importance of giving time and thought to arriving at short term and long range objectives for one's self as well as for an organization.

Another very important subject dealt with in this book is the question of priorities with respect to the use of our time, talents and money. Throughout the book, emphasis is also given to quality in one's life and in one's work. Today there is a great lack of excellence in performance not only in business but in the Lord's work. This book would certainly lead one to aim towards higher excellence of performance in all the phases of one's life. I believe it was Dwight Moody who said: "Do all the good you can, to all the people you can, in all the ways you can, and for as long as you can." I believe the reading of this book and the applying of some of the sound suggestions contained therein would help anyone to do a better job of reaching the high objective in the above statement.

HERBERT J. TAYLOR
President, Club Aluminum Products

DO YOU CARE ENOUGH?

No wonder modern man is plagued by boredom when he flees from the drudgery of work to the meaninglessness of leisure.

—ROBERT LEE

WARNING! Adventure ahead! The reader who has already succumbed to the slavery of a stacked desk or accepted mountains of routine work as the "executive's way of life" will want to stop here. For the hardy soul who makes up his mind to take the plunge, some surprises lie ahead. The first is the title of this book. You see, it's really not about the management of time. Time management, in the final analysis, really gets down to management of yourself.

Every way the authors turned in quest of answers relating to time, the trail ended with the individual. It is *what* he does *with* his time that matters most. He cannot delay the clock or hasten it. He cannot buy time or give it away. He has exactly as much as everyone else. Chaplin Tyler describes it as "the most inexorable and inelastic element in our existence." No respecter of persons or position, the minute hand moves relentlessly on. The difference always turns out to be the individual—how he plans, how he organizes, how he directs, how he controls not only his own activities but the actions of those for whom he is responsible. That's what this book is all about . . . not managing *time,* but managing *your activities* with respect to time.

This is the age of the "harried executive." The Christian in a position of management, to whom this book is dedicated, generally recognizes that he is caught in the throes of a management revolution. Modernization of equipment and introduction of new procedures are transforming his working environment. Data-processing is creating an information explosion which threatens to engulf him. Conferences and seminars flourish as managers and supervisors, an estimated three-quarters of a million annually, pursue an oft-times desperate search of answers.

But has the pressure of time blurred our perspective? Does the struggle to keep up dim our vision? Are we slaves to cluttered desks? Are we so "crisis-oriented" that "opportunities" pass by unrecognized? For most of us the answers to these questions must be affirmative. But how much do we care? Does our general state of disorganization matter enough to make us determined to do something about it? We already know many things we ought to do about it. But, as one sage observer put it, we don't *do* what we *know*.

If personal considerations do not suffice, however, to impel us to begin this adventure into the management of time, what about our concern for responsible stewardship? Can we settle for anything less than the best in the matter of how we utilize those precious resources, including time, which God has entrusted to our care?

If you are faint of heart, stop here. If you think you'd like to improve your use of time but aren't really *committed* to the idea, perhaps you should save your time for less challenging tasks. But if you are one of those few described by Paul Elmen who, in their eagerness for life, cast about for some expression equal to their desire,[1] and listen to One who has said, "I am come that ye might have life, and have it more abundantly," this book may be for you. It is for the harried, but stouthearted . . . for the burdened but determined . . . for the overextended Christian executive who cares enough about his situation to change it—beginning with himself.

TED W. ENGSTROM
R. ALEC MACKENZIE

REFERENCE

[1]—Elmen, Paul, *The Restoration and Meaning to Contemporary Life,* Doubleday and Company, 1958.

CONTENTS

PART THREE: MANAGING OTHERS

PART ONE

There is an astonishing contrast between the heavy perplexity that inhibits before the adventure has begun and the excitement that grips us the moment it begins. . . . As soon as a man makes up his mind to take the plunge into adventure, he is aware of a new strength he did not think he had, which rescues him from all his perplexities.

—Paul Tournier
The Adventure of Living

A PERSPECTIVE ON WORK, TIME AND LEISURE

BOREDOM has become more than a specter on the horizon of modern man. As the work-week shortens and time-saving equipment proliferates, the great majority of America's working force begin to confront a strange dilemma—what to do with the time they have fought so hard to obtain. A group of distinguished news commentators was asked, in an end-of-the-year roundup, what was the gravest crisis facing the American people in the year ahead. After responses ranging from cold-war tensions to the emerging African nations, it came Eric Sevareid's turn to comment. In contrast to the others, Sevareid cited as the most dangerous threat to American society the rise of leisure and the fact that those who have the most leisure are the least equipped to make use of it.[1]

At the other end of the spectrum are the conclusions of the Twentieth Century Fund study by Sebastian de Grazia referring to "our work-centered, almost work-compulsive society." "What is work? What is time? What is leisure?" asks de Grazia. Do the questions startle? Aren't the answers obvious? Be assured, concludes the author, they are not:

> A great fracture in the ethos has taken place. The resultant fault will bring work and time under survey. The American will have to question his identity and ask about his destiny.

13

Why does he work and rush? For bread? To stay alive? Why stay alive? Anyway, does it matter? What really does matter? A great shifting of substrata is going on, a whole pattern of duties and pleasures seeking to come to rest on something new. Work and time's displacement will bring a fresh inclination. Were our traditions of leisure stronger, we could be more confident that it would settle us where we should have been long ago—in the second stage of political community, the living of a life of good quality.[2]

Time is divided between work and leisure. One man's work is another's leisure. Another man's leisure is one man's work. Some men work for pleasure, others solely for profit. Some achieve both. The man whose philosophy is that anything worth doing is worth doing well is more contented in his job. And he will be the man most interested in the subject of the management of time—and himself.

REFERENCES

[1]—Lee, Robert, *Religion and Leisure in America*, Abingdon Press, Nashville, 1964.
[2]—de Grazia, Sebastian, *Of Time, Work and Leisure*, Twentieth Century Fund, New York, 1962.

CHAPTER 1

WHY WORK?

The meaning of man's work is the satisfaction of the instinct for adventure that God has implanted in his heart.

—Paul Tournier

"THERE ARE PEOPLE," says Paul Tournier, "who go on indefinitely preparing for life instead of living it." In his recent book *The Adventure of Living,*[1] this eminent Swiss physician and psychiatrist takes a penetrating look at "the meaning of work." The charm of being an amateur, which Tournier hopes all his life to be, lies in the love that goes into it. It is work done not for gain but for love.

Disenchantment with work is not a new phenomenon. At the turn of the century Arnold Bennett concluded that in the majority of instances man does not precisely feel a passion for his business; and at best he does not like it. He begins his business functions with some reluctance, as late as he can, and he ends them with joy, as early as he can. And his engines, while he is engaged in his business, according to Bennett, are seldom at their full "h.p."[2]

Dr. Tournier finds that most people in our day do not love their work. The resulting serious dissatisfaction with life can lead to many ordinary illnesses. Extraneous pleasures, though numerous, are rarely sufficient to make up for real love of one's work. "To help a worker discover a fresh attraction in his daily work," says the author, "is to help him live a fuller and very often a healthier life."[3]

But the problem of one's attitude toward his work may yield to a more direct approach. Bruce Larson faces the

15

issue squarely: "If you are miserable or bored in your work
. . . or dread going to it . . . then God is speaking to you.
He either wants you to change the job you are in—or—more
likely—He wants to change *you*."[4]

Behavioral scientists, as will be seen in greater detail
later, are making serious inroads on the traditional managerial concepts of organization which will have long-term
effects on the jobs men hold. But perhaps Tournier says it
better than they, holding that in the organization of work,
fruitful reform might well take the idea of the importance
of the person as a starting point. "When a worker believes
that he is looked upon merely as a tool of production, he
feels he is becoming just a thing. When he feels that an
interest is taken in him as a person, in his personal life, in
the adventure of his life, that what is expected of him is
not just a mechanical gesture but a personal understanding
of his work, intelligence, initiative and lively imagination,
as well as a sense of being one of a team engaged in a
common adventure, he takes cognizance of himself as a
person, engaged in a personal adventure."[5]

The author goes on to describe what might happen if
the leaders of industry seriously sought to share with their
workers their over-all view of the adventure in which they
are engaged. Instead the workers are generally left with
the most logical alternative—a concept of their work as an
economic necessity, a means of earning a living. An
individual worker, however well-intentioned he may be as
he attempts to do his best at his own section of work, may
well lose the feeling that his work has any true
significance. Without the over-all picture and a sense of
direction in a unified effort, his work will lapse into
routine. Leaders somehow fail to realize how much the
normal worker can grasp of the big picture, and how much
he needs to know for a basic sense of contribution and
fulfillment.

Dr. Tournier views the questioning young person today
with sympathy. When he asks why it is necessary to work,
it is not enough, the author says, to answer, "Because it is
your duty." "More human than their parents," says Dr.
Tournier, "are those who today are no longer content to
live without thinking, to do everything unintelligently like
everyone else without knowing why."

Nor is the answer to deify work—to say, as some have

concluded, "My work is my life," without understanding its true significance. Man's true value will not be restored to him by deifying or denigrating work, but by helping him to rediscover its true human significance.

Dorothy Sayers points to work as "a way of life in which the nature of man should find its proper exercise and delight and so fulfill itself to the glory of God."⁶ It is a creative activity that should be undertaken for the love of work itself. "Man, made in God's image," continues Miss Sayers, "should make things as God makes them, for the sake of doing well a thing that is well worth doing." It is evident that this standard applies to the work that Christians do, whatever their calling or vocation. "Work," she concludes, "is not primarily a thing one does to live, but the thing one lives to do." It is, or should be, the full expression of the worker's faculties, the thing in which he finds spiritual, mental, social and bodily satisfaction, and the medium in which he offers himself to God.

The consequences of this conclusion, Miss Sayers readily admits, are somewhat revolutionary:

(1) Effort expended must find its true reward not in pay but merely in sufficient return to enable the worker to carry on the work properly, for his work is the measure of his life. Satisfaction comes in the fulfillment of his own nature and in contemplation of the perfection of his work. Witness the loving labor happily put into hobbies, in which the worker no longer bargains with his work, but serves it.

(2) Every man should do the work for which he is fitted by nature. Economic pressure leads an unwitting society to ridicule the man who foregoes a high-paying job for work for which he feels himself better suited. Imagine a purely vocational approach to the business of fitting together the worker and his work. Ed Janis was telling the Dale Carnegie class about one of the most satisfying experiences of his life. He had a well-paying sales job with a nationally known firm. Pressure for increased sales at work began to make a difference at home. Life had somehow become tense. One day Ed decided that it was one thing for him to pay the price of climbing the ladder to success (whatever that was)—but it was another for his family to do so. He found a job that paid less and also put him under less pressure. His prospective boss said, "You'll not make as

much money with us, Ed, but I believe you will be happy here. We're easy to live with." Ed now views his decision to take the new job as one of the most important and one of the best of his life.

(3) We should no longer think of work as something we hasten to finish in order to enjoy our leisure; leisure rather becomes the period of changed rhythm that refreshes us for the delightful purpose of getting on with our work. Thus no regulations would be tolerated which prevented us from working as long and as well as our enjoyment of work demanded. Such restrictions would be resented as a monstrous interference with our liberty. (Miss Sayers leaves to our conjecture the great upheaval of ideas this view could cause in relation to hours of work and rates of pay!) The fight thus would be not for precious hours saved *from* the job—but rather for precious time to get on with the job!

(4) We should fight, tooth and nail, not for mere employment, but for the quality of the work we have to do. We should clamor to be engaged in work that is worth doing and in which we can take pride.

The first of the foregoing propositions concerns workers as such; the second concerns Christians and leads to the firm conclusion that secular vocations are sacred and that time spent working is time spent serving God. The worker must be able to serve God *in* his work, and the work itself must be accepted and respected as the medium of divine creation. This is an important concept for Christians to bear in mind, not only respecting their own vocations, but those of their friends and associates. This concept could make a great difference in the way a Christian executive approached an interview with a prospective employee currently employed in a secular business.

Thus it is clear that in speaking of a Christian view of the management of time, we speak in reality not only of management of ourselves, but we speak also of managing our efforts and endeavors *in whatever vocation we find ourselves as Christians*.

Lest the reader conclude that this view of work is fine if you happen to be a Christian, but that in industry the position would necessarily be opposed, listen to J. D. Batten, of Batten and Associates, who has written extensively in the field of management and conducted many management seminars in this country and abroad. Under sponsorship of the American Management Association he writes:

> Life without productive work directed toward some purpose is meaningless, sterile and messy.... The story has often been told how Wernher von Braun, the great rocket scientist, once flunked a course in mathematics. At that time, he had no particular objective but to finish school, but eventually he began to read about rockets and space, decided this would be his field, and learned how necessary mathematics would be. He then proceeded to take all the mathematics he could in order to reach his target. In the end, he discovered a real zest and pleasure in tackling the roughest problems.
>
> It is imperative that we cease to regard work as a means to an end—a chore to be disposed of so we can enjoy ourselves. Productive, result-oriented work should be viewed in its proper perspective as an integrated, essential and pleasant part of living.[7]
>
> Time after time, men who have reached or are approaching retirement express keen regret at having wasted many productive years in dreams of ease and leisure. They realize belatedly that the opportunity to live richly and fully—to experience the pleasures that can come only with accomplishment—has passed them by.[7]

Again, Ruth Anshen, in introducing the Credo Series' *The Challenge of the Passing Years—My Encounter with Time,* declared the hope of the series "to demonstrate the sacramental character of work." No work, she concluded, "can be based on material, technological or physical aspirations alone."

So we return to the question "Why work?" The Christian executive who works himself and has others working under his supervision must have an answer. The answer to this question should be his philosophy of work. To have such a philosophy is important to every Christian, whether manager or worker; whether husband or housewife. After all, why work? If the average person in a fifty-year work-span spends 100,000 hours working, it should not be asking too much that he know why he is doing so.

REFERENCES

[1]—Tournier, Paul, *The Adventure of Living*, Harper and Row, New York, 1965.

[2]—Bennett, Arnold, *How to Live on 24 Hours a Day*, George H. Doran Company, New York, 1910.

[3]—*Op. cit.*

[4]—Larson, Bruce, *Dare to Live Now*, Zondervan Publishing House, Grand Rapids, 1965.

[5]—*Ibid.*

[6]—Sayers, Dorothy L., *Creed or Chaos?*, Methuen and Company, Ltd., London, 1954.

[7]—Batten, J. D., *Tough-Minded Management*, American Management Association, New York, 1963.

CHAPTER 2

WHAT IS TIME?

For what is Time? Who is able easily and briefly to explain it? Who is able so much as in thought to comprehend it so as to express himself concerning it? And yet what in our usual discourse do we more familiarly and knowingly make more mention of than Time? And surely we understand it well enough when we speak of it; we understand it also when in speaking with another we hear it named. What then is Time? If nobody asks me I know; but if I were desirous to explain it to someone that should ask me, plainly I know not.

—St. Augustine

THE CONFUSION over concepts of time appears from the foregoing quotation clearly not to be of recent origin. Henry Dobson's brief lines in *The Paradox of Time* captured a part of it:

Time goes, you say? Ah, no!
Alas, Time stays, we go.[1]

Perhaps the concept of work as described in the preceding chapter aided Robert MacIver in directing his philosophical thrusts toward the puzzling matter of time. Whatever the reason, this world-renowned political and social scientist notes that time, like space, is a dimension rather than a force. He discerningly observes that time as measured by the clock or calendar is not adequate to many of man's needs. Man may be victimized by clock time, but the real difference, according to the author, is between time *measured* and time *lived*.[3]

Time as measured is the enemy of time as lived. Of the various ways in which we become victims of time perhaps the most obvious is when the work we do is denuded of interest for us. How important our view of work becomes at this point. At once comes to mind the picture of the schoolboy squirming for the closing bell, the office worker with thought only for the evening's coming activities, the machine operator listlessly pursuing prescribed routine, the lawyer dutifully preparing a dull brief for a case that leaves him cold.

Having seen how much our use of time may depend upon our view of our work, let us consider a few of the common misconceptions about time.

Some Misconceptions

In the lives of busy executives there is no question asked more often than "Where has the time gone?" Does it seem strange that the question most often asked, rhetorically to be sure, should so misstate the case? Does time depart the scene, as the question suggests? Or has it simply passed at the rate it always has while we accomplished far less than we should? Or, perhaps, are we really asking, "How could I have planned so poorly and have left so much to be done in so little time?"

"Time is money and must be spent wisely," we have been told all our lives. But have we any choice *not* to spend it? Of course we do not. The hands of the clock move onward inexorably. We have no control over their speed of flight. We may "stop the clock" on a basketball court or on a football field—but never in the game of life.

The sundial's shadow and the sands in the hourglass mean something more than a commodity to be controlled or dispensed at will. So we speak of the ravages of time . . . a hand that cannot be stayed . . . a scythe with which an old man levels all. But is time really a force to be so dreaded, or does it in fact create nothing . . . destroy nothing?

Faith Baldwin called time a seamstress specializing in

alterations. But we know that rocks wear down and stars grow dim, men age and empires decay, *not* because time works on them but because of the ebb and flow of energy systems operating within the physical laws of the universe established by God. If space is the dimension in which things exist, why not accept time, as Robert MacIver suggests, as the dimension in which things change?

"Time flies!" we exclaim—when we mean that we have not accomplished the results expected within the time available.

"Time will take care of it," we say—instead of asserting that the condition will undoubtedly rectify itself, given adequate time.

"I don't have the time," we protest—instead of admitting that the proposal is not sufficiently important in our priorities to warrant *taking* the time for it. We always make time for things that are important enough.

We talk about "the tyranny of time," ascribing to it a capability of acting instead of recognizing it as a measurement of too large a number of tasks to be performed within the time available.

After all, time isn't money or even a commodity; it's not going anywhere ... can't be speeded up or slowed down; it can't be bought or bartered; it's not a ravaging force of evil or an inscrutable judge or an omniscient healer. It is, as Webster put it simply, "the period during which action or process continues." Like sands in the hourglass, so are the days of our lives.

Responsible Stewardship

Surprised by our lack of perception as to the true nature of time, we may well be startled as we contemplate the significance of its equal distribution. When God chose to create us, along with life itself came His gift to all the world. We have the same amount of time in every day as everyone else has. Whether paperboy or president ... author or housewife ... farmer or financier ... the clocks we buy run at the same rate. We have ... whoever we are and wherever we be ... the same number of minutes in our hours as everyone everywhere has. *No one has any more time than you!*

With a clear philosophy of work as a foundation, and a view of time and its management that is closely related to our view of work, our focus on the "stewardship of time" sharpens. We are here to work within God's divine purpose. Among the resources granted for the task, whatever it be, is a fixed amount of time. A Biblical injunction regarding its use is found in Colossians 4:5: "Make the best possible use of your time" (Phillips).

Much is said regarding the stewardship of wealth and possessions. Less is said about stewardship of talent. Little is said concerning stewardship of time. Perhaps even less is understood. What do we mean by being "stewards of our time"? Is it really our time we're talking about, or is it God's time? Has it been granted to us, along with the gift of life itself, to be disposed according to our own purposes . . . with only a portion of our own determining going back to Him from whence it came? Or, as Charles Shedd suggests, since God fashioned the world and all that is in it, does *all* our time *belong to Him?*

Shedd proposes "Ten Affirmations for Christian Use of Time."[3] Appropriately, he begins with purpose: "Life's Single Holy Assignment." From Luke 10:41-42 he draws the parallel of Christ's gentle reminder to Martha that "but one thing is needful." Rather than all her lavish attentions, a simple, quiet talk on heavenly things would have been preferred. A truly effective life, according to Shedd, does not result from getting God to help us. Our lives assume maximum worth when we "turn our wills over to Him and ask that we might be of assistance to His purposes."

Management of time thus becomes, for the Christian, management of His time. And this brings us to what may appear to be a slightly revolutionary thought. When times get out of joint . . . when tasks pile up . . . and when things go wrong . . . how often do we stop to ask God if we're doing what *He* wants us to do? It is *His* time we're managing, isn't *this* where we should begin?

Colleen Townsend Evans has described how this works for her. When life gets just too harried she tries to stop the merry-go-round with the question "Have I pushed Christ out of the center of my life?"[4]

Bruce Larson suggests that "getting our marching orders" can make the difference.[5] Settling the question of whether what we are doing is what *God wants* us to be doing could be the greatest single key to our management of time!

And isn't this Scriptural from yet another perspective—God's promise to supply our every need (Philippians 4:19)?

Surely this must include *time* to *do* the things we ought. Thus the quest for a solution to the problem of better management of time becomes a simple query—"Am I in the center of God's will for my life?" since He has promised to provide the time to do the things I must for Him!

Is TIME the Problem . . . or Are YOU?

Stripped of high-sounding phrases—"a measured piece of eternity"—and common misconceptions—"I had some time on my hands"—we arrive at the conclusion that time is but a measurement . . . a dimension. Hence, *it* can scarcely be our problem. In any query into the matter of time and its management, all roads ultimately lead back to management of ourselves. The entire science of management deals with the way executives allocate their time.

Should this be so startling? Note the similarity in the complaints about time. There just doesn't seem to be enough of it. More precisely, of course, we try to do too much in the time we have available. Remember . . . we have, and always have had, all the time there is!

So the problem is, has been, and will be, not time . . . but ourselves. And, fortunately, we can do something about this.

Before we attack the matter of self-management, let us beware of stumbling over the first hurdle—God's will. We have already observed that our most basic problem with lack of time may well be that we have pushed God out of the center of our lives. We have seen that His promise to provide for all our needs certainly must extend to this most basic element—time. Now, however, we find ourselves in the human arena where God, despite our frailties, has chosen to work. He has endowed us with certain talents and capabilities, each unique, then given each of us the right to choose his own path.

Out of this divinely created relationship, open to whoever would have it, comes the question "How do I know when the path I choose is the one God would have me take?" How do we know when the resources God has placed in our care are being used as He wills them to be? Is there a danger, in matters of organized Christian endeavors, of "overspiritualizing" some problems—where common sense might seem to provide answers—and with respect to other tasks, of somehow "depending on God to get them done" or saying to oneself, "He hasn't told me to do it yet"? Such problems may lead to a distorted sense of "fellowship" which, as we shall see in a later chapter, can render the Lord's work ineffectual and inefficient. Since this cannot be His will, it must not be ours. We approach the matter of managing ourselves, then, from the perspective of being in God's perfect will for our lives . . . of committing our wills to Him . . . of harnessing all our faculties and all the resources He has entrusted to our care to the ultimate purpose He may have for our lives.

REFERENCES

[1]—Dobson, Henry Austin, *The Paradox of Time.*

[2]—MacIver, Robert M., *The Challenge of the Passing Years—My Encounter with Time,* Simon and Schuster, 1962 (Lieber Professor of Political Philosophy and Sociology, Columbia University, 1927-1950).

[3]—Shedd, Rev. Charles W., *Time for All Things,* Abingdon Press, 1962.

[4]—Evans, Colleen T., "My Family Comes First," *Guideposts,* November, 1965.

[5]—*Op. cit.*

CHAPTER 3

WHAT IS LEISURE?

There is no music in a "rest" but there's the making of music in it. And people are always missing that part of the life melody.

—John Ruskin

WHEN we asked ourselves, in Chapter 1, the question "Why Work?" we began by suggesting that as Christians, particularly Christian executives, we were long overdue for a closer look at work. "Now," you ask, "what about leisure?" Yes, indeed . . . what about it? "Pray tell," the "harried" executive pleads in mock surprise, "will someone *show* me some?"

What about executives who talk of leisure as if it were some dim and distant promised land . . . who speak of it in yearning terms as if it were to be highly sought after though virtually unattainable? Do they really want it? Do they know what it is? Could they put it to meaningful use if they had it? Many observers believe that most executives answer these questions in the negative.

If this were not so, why haven't they taken it? Why hasn't the group which has wrung the highest monetary rewards from the economic system . . . the one group which *could* have more leisure time if it *wanted* it . . . why hasn't this group arranged to have it?

Why Executives Choose Long Hours

What begins to seem obvious, though who would state it so bluntly, is that executives work long hours by choice! Clarence Randall had little patience with the poor, harried, overworked manager:

27

Pity the overworked executive! Behind his paperwork ramparts, he struggles bravely with a seemingly superhuman load of responsibilities. Burdened with impossible assignments, beset by constant emergencies, he never has a chance to get organized. Pity him—but recognize him for the dangerous liability that he is.[1]

Randall views as self-appointed martyrs, these Horatios, convinced of their pivotal responsibility, their sacrificial effort, their monumental contribution to the organization. Almost every organization has them. You will know them by their messy desks (too busy to straighten it) . . . by papers strewn in disarray (*all* important papers come to *this* desk) . . . by the hasty sandwich brought in by a harried secretary (too much can go wrong if a man this important is away from his desk too long) . . . by the bulging brief case lugged out the door after everyone else has gone (who knows, some late workman might see it and rejoice that *someone* cares enough about the work to worry about it after hours) . . . by the quick kiss for wife upon late arrival home and the query "Why isn't dinner ready?" (important people must never be kept waiting) . . . by the unopened brief case lugged back in the morning (late enough to be seen by those who missed it the night before) . . . by that vacation he "hasn't taken in fifteen years" (how grateful to "old faithful" the directors must be—what other chair in the office has been warmed so uninterruptedly over so long a period of time?) . . . by the rushing off on urgent trips (a phone call might offend the receiver of so important a message) . . . by the endless list of routine tasks (who would think of delegating when there is just no one who could do them quite as well?) . . . by his chronic late arrival at conferences (with an air of preoccupation suggesting how generous he is to take time for lesser matters) . . . by his inability to meet deadlines (but his readiness with a reason why, inevitably associated with the gargantuan task he stands astride).

"Leisure time?" you ask. Oh, yes, leisure time. Perhaps we'd better back up a bit. Can the harried executive we've just described possibly have a meaningful "philosophy of work"? If he has no philosophy of work, can he possibly have a philosophy of leisure? If work, as Dorothy Sayers proposes, is not the thing one does to live, but is rather the thing one lives to do, we find here our springboard to an understanding of leisure.

Executives, and Christian executives without a doubt, live to work. The combination of commitment, dedication and opportunity to serve God and fellow man provides tremendous motivation. Even more than other executives, Christians find the lines between work and leisure blurred. The executive enjoys a freedom to come and go not enjoyed by clerical, office and and shop workers. He schedules himself . . . enjoys lunch with others of his choosing for purposes of business, to be sure, but enjoyable nonetheless. The freedom to move where the action is . . . to delegate to others . . . to contemplate the future . . . to plan to take advantage of opportunity . . . to see dreams come true . . . this is work? Indeed. This, for many, is also leisure—the optimum fulfillment of the heart's desire when God's hand reveals itself throughout.

All of this, according to Sebastian de Grazia,[2] is why executives choose long hours, and are therefore less to be pitied than we think. If the executive himself realized the extent to which his work is interlaced with qualities normally associated with voluntary, carefree and social pursuits, he would feel less sorry for himself.

But the Christian executive has a built-in rationalization since normally underfinanced endeavors cannot afford adequate staffs. No better excuse has been found for overwork than lack of adequate staff. The reader is cautioned to review for himself what the real reason or reasons for his own situation may be. The distinct possibility has now been raised that, in fact, you may not be so overworked as you would like to think—and that if you are, it may well be because you want it that way. Should *either* of these possibilities be true, think of the tension which can be avoided by a simple reminder of the fact! Martyrdom that is self-invited somehow does seem less respectable.

What then of leisure? If work is God-ordained . . . if it is what we live to do . . . then leisure acquires a purposefulness of its own. It becomes a time of self-renewal, of re-creation of our energies and talents and capabilities for the joyful pursuit of what we are called to do . . . be it Christian or secular.

At a time when the "great American dream" is catapulting our nation down the primrose path of abundance . . . of electronic accessories . . . of undreamed of timesavers, which cost money, which must be paid for by money which takes more time to earn ... philosophers are asking if we know where we are going. Do we appreciate the difference between leisure and free time? Are we even capable of using leisure in a meaningful way if we had it?

Among the compulsions that drive busy executives must surely be this gnawing uncertainly about what to do with leisure. With all of the guilt complexes Christians have constructed, one or two must apply to use of leisure time. Is it Christian, for instance, to loaf? How does this great American pastime fit into a philosophy of the stewardship of time?

We've agreed that each of us has all the time there is, and that it all came as a gift from God. If it's God's time we're dealing with, what then of leisure? The perspective seems a bit clearer. We are here for His purposes ... we are doing the task He ordained for us ... our leisure belongs to Him ... and, amazingly, He is more available to us than busy executives are.

> Executives are hard to see;
> Their costly time I may not waste;
> I make appointments nervously
> And talk to them in haste.
> But at any time of night or day,
> In places suitable or odd,
> I seek and get without delay
> An interview with God.
> —Anonymous[3]

Leisure for God's purposes seems much more meaningful than leisure for the sake of leisure. It also aids us in our concept of managing our time. The harried manager may now see more reason to break the stranglehold of his habits ... when a vacation with his family, postponed for five years, can be viewed as God's plan not only for his family's sake but for his own. An opportunity for active participation in a civic undertaking for which his talents suit him admirably may make him a far more effective manager on the job. A change of pace, while expending effort in a new direction, can be wonderfully refreshing, particularly for desk-bound executives. And for the Christian, the question of whether his "hurried state" is God-imposed or man-imposed may well be worth reflecting upon. "Our heavenly Father," observes Charles Shedd, "never gives us too much to do. Men will. We assign ourselves an overload, but never the Lord. He knows what He wants from each of us, and there is plenty of time in His day for things essential to His plan. We do Him a grave injustice when we fall into the habit of compulsive overwork. We sin when we pressure out His wishes for assignments that have not been filtered through divine judgment. Self-centered scheduling that wants it our way, and ours alone, is far different from setting up a plan with the Inner Presence as our guide."[4]

With this returning thought of keeping our lives Christ-centered, time enough to do all things seems certain, and the question of leisure time yields itself to the commitment of being true stewards of *all* His time. And what a promise for the time-harried, worry-laden executive who thus claims the promise of Jesus: "These things have I spoken unto you, that my joy might remain in you, and that your joy might be full" (John 15:11).

REFERENCES

—Randall, Clarence B., *The Folklore of Management*, Little, Brown and Company, Boston, 1961.

[2]—de Grazia, Sebastian, *Of Time, Work and Leisure*, Twentieth Century Fund Study.

—Shedd, Rev. Charles W., *Time for All Things*, Abingdon Press, Nashville, 1962.

[4]—*Ibid.*

PART TWO

A PERSPECTIVE ON
MANAGING YOURSELF

Unless he manages himself effectively, no amount of ability, skill, experience or knowledge will make an executive effective.

—Peter Drucker

THE EDITORS of *Nation's Business* have compiled a carefully selected compendium of articles of particular interest to executives. Now in its third edition under the title of "Three Steps to More Skillful Management," this compendium consists of three groups of articles, the first of which is titled "Managing Yourself." The other two fall under the titles "Managing Your People" and "Managing Your Business."

In the lead article, Peter Drucker, one of our nation's foremost corporation consultants, discusses five ways to become a more effective executive: (1) Focus effort on fewer jobs; (2) Eliminate the obsolete; (3) Learn how you spend your time; (4) Avoid unproductive decisions; and (5) Test ideas. He concludes by reminding the reader that while books on management talk about managing the work of others, one can really be certain of managing only himself. And unless he does this effectively, cautions Drucker, no amount of ability, skill, experience or knowledge will make him an effective executive.

Francois Rabelais likewise emphasized self-management: "How shall I be able to rule over others if I have not full power and command of myself?"[1]

But there is a pardox involved at this point for the Christian who comprehends man's inability to control his own nature. Dr. Walter Judd summarizes this predicament and its solution: "Man is so smart today; he controls almost all of nature—except his own nature; For that he needs a Saviour. That Saviour is available."[2]

REFERENCES

[1]—Rabelais, Francois, *Works*, Chap. 52.

[2]—Judd, Walter H., "Critique on Conflict," *Collegiate Challenge*, Vol. 5, No. 1.

CHAPTER 4

SOCRATES SAYS "KNOW THYSELF"
—DO YOU?

All about us today are examples of executives struggling to solve problems of the 1960's with the management tools of the 1930's.

—George Frank

Rate Your Skills

Much has been written about the self-appraisal of his own skills by the executive. Since we have established that the problem of time-management is really a problem of self-management with respect to time, a close look at ourselves is in order. Realistic self-appraisal is not easy. The less secure one feels in his position the less inclined he will be to pursue this course of action. But there are many available tools to aid the executive in mirroring his own strengths and weaknesses. One of the best-known aids to self-appraisal is found in the popular helpful book *The Efficient Executive* by Auren Uris.[1] This "Skills Rating Chart," as it is called, divides twenty-one executive skills into three basic categories: *human relation* skills (working with subordinates and maintaining good relations with your superior); *procedural or administrative* skills (control of paperwork and using work time effectively); and *personal* skills (memory and concentration).

Through the courtesy of Research Institute of America, this chart is reproduced to enable the reader to rate himself and to compare his rating with the "average" profile from a group of 143 executives. Your analysis may reveal a general area of strengths or weaknesses which should be exploited or, alternatively, given special attention for improvement. The extent to which these skills are used on relatively important tasks will affect your decision as to which are worthy of special effort.

Some executives, doubting their ability to appraise themselves objectively, have done their own rating and also had one of their associates rate them for comparative purposes.

In evaluating areas for emphasis, caution should be exercised before concluding that low scores necessarily signal the most productive targets for attention. To hope to score uniformly high on all executive skills is unrealistic. In a later chapter on "delegation" we will see that one of the greatest benefits of effective delegation is the optimum utilization of special talents on the management team. Thus, should you chance to rate low in an area where a subordinate is strong, it probably would be the wiser course to delegate. Your subordinate thus can perform in his area of strength, leaving you free also to move in areas of strength.

SKILLS RATING CHART

Low Medium High

	Low	Medium	High
1. *Using the expert*—getting information, opinions, ideas from well-informed people inside or outside your company.	—	—	—
2. *Building reputation*—making yourself known; developing a favorable name for yourself in the company.	—	—	—
3. *Activating*—getting your people to understand and follow your instructions.	—	—	—
4. *Imparting information*—making yourself understood by subordinates or superiors.	—	—	—
5. *Judging people*—gauging individuals so as to be able to establish good relations and increase job perfection.	—	—	—
6. *Working with subordinates*—establishing cordial and effective relationships with those who work with you.	—	—	—
7. *Interviewing*—talking with people face to face.	—	—	—
8. *Listening*—learning from the words of others how they think and feel.	—	—	—

Low Medium High

9. *Getting information*—motivating people to join you in accomplishing departmental goals. — — —

10. *Maintaining good relationships with your superior*—being both friendly and businesslike in your dealings up the line. — — —

11. *Using time effectively*—being able to get sixty minutes of work out of every hour. — — —

12. *Decision-making*—arriving at a logical conclusion and sticking to it. — — —

13. *Planning*—developing a course of action to accomplish a definite objective. — — —

14. *Controlling paperwork*—maintaining the flow of interoffice communications, reports and the like, to and from your desk. — — —

15. *Getting information*—uncovering the facts you need to advance your work. — — —

16. *Delegation*—making subordinates responsible for some of your activities, while retaining control. — — —

17. *Problem-solving*—licking the tough situations that interfere with efficiency. — — —

18. *Pacing your energy expenditures*—conserving yourself so as to be able to complete the day without undue fatigue. — — —

19. *Concentration*—being able to stick with a given task. — — —

20. *Memory*—remembering events, incidents, ideas, plans or promises. — — —

21. *Self-scheduling*—accomplishing the objectives of your job by efficient allotment of your time. — — —

Recognizing the innate resistance to self-appraisal which all humans face, Howard Dresser devised a somewhat unique approach. Reminding his reader that it is not hard to criticize another person's work, he suggests thinking about an associate and asking these questions regarding his performance: (1) Can he be relied upon to do what he says he will do? (2) Does he meet deadlines? (3) Does he make his own decisions? (4) Does he check facts carefully? (5)

Does he make good use of his time? Realizing the ease with which one answers these questions regarding an associate, we quickly see the ease with which they ought to be answered regarding our own performance.

Test Your Weakness

Until recently the term "managerial obsolescence" has been given no more than scant attention. Today the term is common talk in seminars and conferences . . . in books and articles . . . wherever the problems of management are discussed. The computer has done a great deal to prompt the panic. With vastly increased volumes of data suddenly available to the management team, new emphases are inevitable. New and persuasive theories of management generated by concentrated efforts of behavioral scientists present managers with concepts to be understood and evaluated in the light of their situations. Just as managers in industry face a difficult task in "keeping up" with new trends in managerial thinking, so with those who hold similar positions in Christian organizations. The latter, in fact, may face an even more critical problem, if no serious effort has been made to acquire a basic understanding of the principles of management at the outset.

Not infrequently Christian organizations are headed by dynamic individuals with forceful personalities. Called "entrepreneurs" in managerial parlance, these strong and often charismatic leaders provide the vision, initiative and determination to "break through the barriers and get the mission going." As the organization grows to maturity . . . as the staff grows from two or three to sometimes hundreds . . . as the budget doubles and doubles again . . . as the capital assets multiply . . . it is clear that the *needs* of the organization are *changing*. What the changing organization begins to require is management of a going endeavor rather than opening of new frontiers . . . solidifying of the work rather than possible overextension of resources.

Happy is the man, and blessed is the organization, where this has been recognized. Entrepreneurs make the best managers, insists Louis A. Allen, a leading consultant, after a study of 385 companies involving more than 12,000 managers.[2] Virtually every one of the large industries, according to Allen, outgrew their founders, or, if they were fortunate, had leaders who recognized this critical fact of life in their organization's growth.

So "managerial obsolescence" may come about simply as a result of the changing needs of a growing organization, if not as a result of the technological revolution or new developments in management thinking.

In *The Menace of Management Obsolescence,* George Frank describes the enormous changes and rate of change in business operations in the last decade.[2] He concludes that the costly obsolescence of management personnel has shifted from a gnawing problem to an alarming one. He calls, among other things, for policies and programs of management development that will help managers keep abreast of new techniques by demanding of them the same familiarity with up-to-date thinking that is required of hourly workers.

The author cites growing evidence that management is becoming "imperfectly developed, atrophied, suppressed or lacking," to borrow from the dictionary definition of obsolescence. The study of his own company confirmed some startling conclusions about managers: (1) They tend to use progressively less of their training and stop learning new ideas and new techniques when they leave the campus. (2) They practice management mechanically, lacking dynamic interest in management as a profession. (3) They exhibit little familiarity with advanced management techniques—they judge the average management practitioner to be as well acquainted with new methods as he is with Sanskrit. (4) They show little appreciation of the fact that many aspects of business management are evolving toward a science rather than a seat-of-the-pants operation. And (5) they barely recognize the advances made by the social sciences in such areas as communications, participation, motivation and other humanistic aspects of the business enterprise.

Frank's company lists a number of new management tools in a questionnaire for its management personnel recruiting, as follows:

MANAGEMENT SELF-ANALYSIS

Please make a fair self-evaluation about your knowledge in the following areas. Can you apply and do you understand—

From the field of economics:
  Present discounted capital?
  National income statistics?
  Leading and concurrent economic indicators?
  Marginal productivity?

From the field of finance:
  Turnover ratios?
  Retirement and replacement programs?
  Cost of money?
  Rate of return?
  Present value of money?

From the field of marketing:
  The design and evaluation of surveys and questionnaires?
  The design of a consumer panel?
  Survey-sampling design?
  Market penetration analysis?
  Analytical forecast of sales?

From the field of organization:
  Responsibility charting?
  Formal versus informal organization?
  Organization-planning?
  Management audit?

From the field of personnel:
  A design of a job evaluation system?
  A wage and salary survey and wage regression curve?
  Executive compensation-planning?
  Programmed instruction?

From the field of operations research:
  Linear programming?
  Inventory models?
  Economic order points?
  Queueing?

From the field of integrated data-processing:
  Computer language?
  Computer-diagramming and flow-charting?
  Random access storage?
  Digital versus analog computers?

From the field of statistics:
  General probability, descriptive and inference statistics?
  Analysis of variance?

Product-moment correlation?
A Chi-square analysis?

From the field of industrial engineering:
A ratio delay or work-sampling study?
I. E. Schematic models?
CPM and PERT?
A work simplification program?
A production cost analysis?
An evaluation of the pros and cons of process versus product-controlled layout?
An incentive system installation?

Frank refers to the "destructive costs" of a management team virtually ignorant of current management science and techniques. Such costs can be assessed directly and indirectly. A large number of decisions on expenditures are made by these managers. They decide manpower and inventory levels as well as patterns of distribution. They make decisions on purchase of materials or equipment, engineering, and make-or-buy alternatives.

In his strong plea for a new look at management development, the author insists that industry today can no longer afford to settle for mediocre performance from its managers. Holding that management is simply not measuring up to its opportunities, he calls that result "destruction-by-inertia of human resources." Christian organizations have much to learn from industry . . . and from its critics such as George Frank.

REFERENCES
—Uris, Auren, *The Efficient Executive,* McGraw-Hill, New York, 1957.
—Allen, Louis A., *The Management Profession,* McGraw-Hill, New York, 1964.
—Frank, George, *The Menace of Management Obsolescence, The Job in a Changing World,* American Management Association, New York, 1964.

CHAPTER 5

WHERE ARE YOU HEADING?

We can know whether what we are doing is absurd only after we have identified the goals we are trying to achieve.

—Charles Hughes

What Results Are You Supposed to Accomplish?

IT IS TIME to take a look at your job. What results are you expected to achieve? If you have a job description, is it spelled out in terms of activities or results? If the former, can you make the conversion to results? If no position description exists, try writing one paragraph to describe all of your responsibilities.

Christian psychologist Henry Brandt asks the questions "Where do you want to go in life? How do you want to get there? Do the roles you fill contribute to your goal? What is really important that you do? What merely fills up time?" He says further, "In determining your best roles you ought to keep those that advance you toward your goal—perhaps even expand one or more if you can and eliminate those that are useless and a drag. Your trouble may be too many good roles. You cannot afford to take on more than you can handle well."

As outlined in the *Manual of Position Descriptions* of the American Management Association,[1] a position guide consists of three items: (1) position description; (2) position qualifications; and (3) organization chart. We are here concerned with the first of these items, the position description. A skeleton outline of a possible position description might look like this:

POSITION DESCRIPTION—GENERAL DIRECTOR
XYZ FELLOWSHIP, INC.

Basic Function

As chief executive officer of XYZ Fellowship, Inc., the General Director is responsible for the general direction of all operations and affairs of the Fellowship as a whole, and for advising and making recommendations to the Board of Directors with respect to these matters.

Responsibilities and Authority

Within the limits of the Articles of Incorporation, Bylaws and policies established or authorized by the Board of Directors, he is responsible for, and has commensurate authority to accomplish, the duties set forth below. He may delegate portions of his responsibilities, consistent with sound operations and authorized policies and procedures, together with proportionate authority for their fulfillment, but he may not delegate or relinquish any portion of his accountability for results.

1. Informs the Board of Directors fully on status and progress of the various activities of the Fellowship and all important factors influencing them, and properly represents the Board to staff members, volunteer workers, donors and the general public.

2. Oversees execution of all decisions of the Board of Directors except when execution is otherwise specified by the Bylaws or by action of the Board of Directors.

3. Directs the development of specific policies, procedures and programs to implement the general policies established by the Board of Directors, and oversees the effective administration and control of these policies, procedures and programs.

4. Evolves appropriate modifications to the over-all objectives of the Fellowship from time to time and secures Board approval for same. Oversees the development of complementary and supportive objectives within the various departmental units of the Fellowship.

5. Develops and recommends to the Board of Directors long-range plans, consistent with the over-all objectives of the Fellowship, and oversees the development of similar planning at appropriate levels throughout the organization.

6. Periodically reviews and evaluates the soundness of the organization structure and the related responsibilities

and authority of key personnel, and effects the changes required to meet changed conditions or improve the operations and effectiveness of the organization and its components.

7. Insures optimum utilization of personnel throughout the Fellowship. To this end, staffs key positions with competent people, delegates appropriate authority, and insures understanding of major assignments. Places appropriate emphasis upon the training and development of leaders to meet present and foreseeable needs. Reviews performance of key personnel on regular basis against developed criteria of performance in relation to established objectives, and takes corrective action where indicated. Recommends salary adjustments annually or more often, as indicated.

8. Develops and implements an appropriate program for public relations and promotion of the work of the Fellowship.

9. Proposes and executes such contracts and commitments as may be authorized by the Board of Directors or by established policies.

10. Develops, gets Board approval for, implements, and controls an appropriate budgetary procedure throughout the Fellowship. Prepares and submits to the Board of Directors an annual consolidated budget for review and approval.

11. Determines that all funds, physical assets and other property of the Fellowship are appropriately safeguarded and administered.

Relationships

The General Director develops and nurtures the following relationships:

1. *Board of Directors*—He is accountable solely to the Board for the administration of the Fellowship and for proper interpretation and fulfillment of his functions, responsibilities, authority and relationships.

2. *Field Staff*—The Regional and Overseas Directors are under his direct supervision. (See paragraph 3 below.)

3. *Administrative Staff*—All Administrative or Department Heads are under his direct supervision. He supervises, coordinates and assists in the activities of each of these offices. He is accountable for the effective performance of each. He secures their advice and assistance in formulating

over-all organization objectives, plans and programs, and stands ready at all times to render them advice, assistance and support.

4. *Donors and Friends*—He represents the Fellowship in an informing and inspiring way to the families of donors and friends.

5. *Others*—He conducts such other relationships as the Board of Directors may specify or as he may deem appropriate and in the best interests of the Fellowship, including those with churches, denominational representatives, seminaries and leaders of other Christian organizations.

What Results Could You Accomplish?

After completion of a position description, such as the one suggested above, the executive should have a picture of "results expected." Next comes the question concerning "results possible." What results, above and beyond those expected, might possibly be accomplished? Remember that in this chapter we are concerned with *reviewing our opportunities.*

In his classic presentation of *Managing a Manager's Time,*[2] William Oncken divides executive duties into three categories: job-imposed; system (organization)-imposed; and self-imposed. He suggests that what sets apart or distinguishes the effective or successful executives is the number, significance and rate of completion of their self-imposed tasks. These are those tasks not called for in the job description . . . not required by the organization . . . but voluntarily assumed by the executive who sees a need and a means of fulfilling it on his own. The manager who thinks in this area—Oncken calls it the "area of ambiguity" due to the lack of guidelines—will be an "opportunity-oriented" manager. Concentration on such areas may offer great potential gains as opposed to concentration on problem areas alone. More will be said about this in Chapter 6.

In considering what *could* be accomplished in your job, again think in terms of results, not activities . . . of accomplishments, not stated duties. If things went right . . . if events transpired in a favorable sequence . . . if resources could be marshalled at the opportune place and moment . . . what *might* be possible? One head of an international Christian organization has found this very question to be of significant help in orienting and directing his entire organizational effort.

In a recent *Guideposts* piece, Dr. Dorothy L. Brown wrote, "Just as God gives each one of us our special talent, so does He give us our dreams to make us aware of the talent."

The Acceptance of Change

Today's executives have developed a keen appreciation for change . . . that is, in matters other than their own jobs. Gaining acceptance of change in organizational policies has become common subject for executive seminars and management publications. New insights from the behavioral sciences have reinforced what may have been long suspected by some: whatever gets done is done through people; to do things better means change; people resist change. Hence the emphasis on winning acceptance of change.

The change in a manager's own job may be so gradual, and so continual, that it is scarcely discernible. Even when sought in any but the most thorough and systematic way, such change may go unrecognized. This makes doubly important the task described above—that of carefully analyzing your own job.

An added benefit in this procedure is the opportunity it presents of comparing your own job requirements with your organizational objectives. If these over-all objectives are in writing, the task is simple. If they are not, write them down, and then compare. If there are aspects of your job which do not coincide with any stated organizational objectives, take a second look at that particular aspect of your job. Why are you doing it? Because your predecessor did it? Because things in the organization have always been done this way? Did an influential member of the Board inaugurate the procedure . . . and is he pretty sticky about suggestions for change? Hopefully, this process will result in redefining, modifying, and especially eliminating many activities done previously without questioning. Then, when your own objectives and job requirements have been trimmed to coincide precisely with the organization objectives, *concentrate* your efforts *on the essentials.* Ray Josephs refers to this as the "instinct for the jugular."[1] No characteristic better describes the critical activity of the successful Christian executive than his conscious application of effort to the strategic requirements of the job.

Plan Your Work

It has been said that time is on the manager's side the moment he organizes it. While the time an executive should spend planning ahead may vary depending on a number of factors, the concensus of consultant opinion is that almost no executives spend *enough* time on this critical area. The higher up the executive ladder one goes, the smaller is the proportion of his time which should be spent on present problems and the greater is the proportion which ought to be spent on future considerations.

Long-Range Planning

In developing the planning function, logic favors starting long-range. Until you know where you want to be at the journey's end, it is difficult to plot the course on a daily or weekly basis. Just as long-range objectives are the most important of all objectives . . . so with planning. While some industries plan up to twenty years ahead, consensus holds that planning for five years ahead is practical for most endeavors.

A realistic approach to developing plans five years ahead is to request from each department or division their five-year expectations of accomplishment. The composite of these divisional goals, discussed and modified as they certainly should be, will provide the basic structure for your long-range plan. General experience has shown that goals set by managers or supervisors for themselves tend to be too high. There appears to be a tendency to want to set the objectives or goals at the highest possible level. Managers and executives face the problem of applying a realistic yardstick to goals which have been set in such a way. That this tendency should almost uniformly result from participative goal-setting is reason enough to practice this method. Other benefits, discussed in a later chapter, include the increased tendency to feel highly motivated to accomplish goals which you have had a part in establishing.

Intermediate-Range Planning

While planning from one to five years ahead may conveniently be termed long-range, that from one month to one year may be termed intermediate-range planning. Once the long-range plans are set, the question is put: "Where must we be in three months ... or six ... or nine ... in order to achieve the long-range objectives in one year?" Thus, by starting with the longest-range objectives, one can work back to the shortest-range objectives. All intermediate requirements which must be met in each division or department, when grouped together, become the intermediate objectives or plans.

Short-Range Planning

We must also consider those requirements which, in order to achieve the intermediate goals, must be accomplished in one day to one month. Whatever must be accomplished within this short span of time in order to achieve the intermediate objectives becomes the short-range plans or objectives.

But, you ask, what happens to the longer-range plans when something goes wrong short-range? A good question. It puts the finger on a point often neglected ... that of flexibility or adjustability of planning. The Critical Path Method tells planners in space and electronics industries what happens "down the line" when a delay is encountered at any point along the path. As actual progress of your plan is plotted against short- and intermediate-range plans, and the deviations between planned and actual performance are visible, these discrepancies should be transferred to the longer-range plans, unless other action is possible to compensate for the loss.

Similarly, every year that passes converts all plans to a minus-one-year basis. Thus the former five-year plan is now the four-year plan, with corrections to accommodate actual performance over the past year. A new five-year plan must be created, based on the best information available at the time.

When to Plan

The most successful planners in Christian service seem to find that a few moments of prayerful, relative quiet at the end of a given period (a day ... or a week) provide the best opportunity for planning the next period. For instance, at the end of the previous afternoon you can write up a calendar page consisting simply of the items to be accomplished on this day. As they are completed, cross them off. As new tasks arise, simply add them to the list. On a good day you may cross off nearly all the items. On a poor day, planning-wise, you may cross off only one or two. But the list is there ... directly in front of you ... a constant reminder of the things to be done *that day*. By stopping at the end of one day to consider what needs to be done the next, you are more likely to think of what really must be accomplished because you are still geared to thinking about the job. Further, once you have written your list for tomorrow, you stand a better chance of being able to leave your problems in the office when you go home, without fear of forgetting them.

Remember that you set long-range objectives first, then intermediate, then short. Thus, in setting daily tasks, you really must know what you planned to accomplish in a given week. These subgoals, those which must be accomplished if the week's goals are to be met, added to the new goals which arise in the course of everyday business, make up the daily targets confronting every manager.

The time chart on page 58 provides space for listing planned accomplishments for the day in which the time is to be recorded. One of the discoveries you will probably make is the underestimation of the time required to accomplish given tasks. The extent of this misjudgment has come as a great surprise to many managers. It is common to misjudge by as much as fifty per cent ... or for a job to require twice as long for completion as originally thought necessary.

This discovery frequently leads to another even more disconcerting—that in terms of results accomplished, far less is done in the typical workday than we ever dreamed. Thus another benefit of the entire procedure arises ... that of resolving to set priorities since so much less is accomplished than we thought ... and that of concentrating on the essentials since we will then be accomplishing the greatest possible results with the effort expended.

Many benefits have been cited by managers who plan ahead for the things they want to accomplish the following day. One perhaps less apparent than others is the avoiding of indecision. Upon arrival at the office and a cluttered desk, what executive has not shrugged his shoulders and wondered where to begin? What executive has not found himself beginning at the top of the stack . . . with whatever item happened, by pure chance, to be on top? Though each of us has, at one time or another, done precisely this, we would not welcome the conclusion that at this very point our job was running us. Yet such a conclusion is inescapable. By writing down the things to be accomplished, and in order of priority, the *indecision* which may be one of the manager's more deadly enemies, and certainly one of his greatest timewasters, can be reduced considerably.

Most students of management are familiar with the incident regarding the remarkable payment of twenty-five thousand dollars for essentially the suggestions presented thus far in this chapter. For the reader who may not have chanced upon the story, it is well worth repeating.

When Charles M. Schwab was president of Bethlehem Steel he confronted Ivy Lee, a management consultant, with an unusual challenge: "Show me a way to get more things done," he demanded. "If it works, I'll pay anything within reason."

Lee handed Schwab a piece of paper. "Write down the things you have to do tomorrow," he said. Schwab did it. "Now number these items in the order of their real importance," Lee continued. Schwab did that. "The first thing tomorrow morning," Lee added, "start working on number one and stay with it until it is completed. Next take number two and don't go any further until it is completed. Then proceed to number three, and so on. If you can't complete everything on schedule, don't worry. At least you will have taken care of the most important things before getting distracted by items of lesser consequence.

"The secret is to do this daily," continued Lee. "Evaluate the relative importance of the things you have to get done . . . establish priorities . . . record your plan of action . . . and stick to it. Do this every working day. After you have convinced yourself of the value of this system, have your men try it. Test it as long as you like. Then send me a check for whatever you think the idea is worth."

In a few weeks Charles Schwab sent Ivy Lee a check for twenty-five thousand dollars. Schwab later said that this lesson was the most profitable one he had ever learned in his business career.

REFERENCES

[1]—Bennett, C. L., *Defining the Manager's Job: The A.M.A. Manual of Position Descriptions,* American Management Association, New York, 1958.

[2]—Oncken, William, *Managing a Manager's Time,* a film, American Management Association, New York, 1961.

[3]—Josephs, Ray, "Control Your Personal Time Better to Get More Done," *American Business,* February, 1960.

CHAPTER 6

HOW ARE YOU DOING?
—ARE YOU ON COURSE?

LOST, yesterday, somewhere between sunrise and sunset, two golden hours, each set with sixty diamond minutes. No reward is offered, for they are gone forever.
                                                    —Horace Mann

IN ORDER to more sharply define the "jugular" target referred to earlier, we turn now to the inventory of our time. Up to this point we have been outlining our responsibilities showing how we *ought* to be spending our time . . . and pin-pointing opportunities indicating how we *could* be investing our time for maximum results. Now we look to see how we are *actually* spending it. Where does the time really go?

This is one of the mythical hurdles said to "separate the men from the boys . . . the managers from the dreamers." The loudest wail ever heard in the executive corridors is that with which the "overworked" manager greets the consultant's decree to inventory his time.

Perhaps this is reasonable, or at least predictable. After all, managers are the people Eric Webster described as "spending their time in a flat spin . . . working up to sixty hours a week, taking work home and then carting it back (often uncompleted) to an office where he'll be interrupted every eight minutes or so—where he'll spend more time talking than thinking—where he'll tend to be run by his job instead of running it—and have about as much mastery over his environment as a table-tennis ball."[1]

But the author of this observation, in another challenging and novel article, advises against the inventory of time.[2] "If Parkinson's Law (work expands to fill the time available) is to be repealed," he argues, "the only way to do it is to eliminate fussy little projects—not add another one such as keeping a laundry list of our activities." To support his point Webster observes that the results of such time studies are depressingly similar. They all boil down to the sad conclusion that (1) you work too long; (2) you don't get enough done; and (3) a lot of what you do should be done by someone else or perhaps not done at all.

"Why, then," you may ask with Eric Webster, "must I take time, the most precious element I possess and the resource in shortest supply, to write down what I do? Isn't the one certain result of this folly going to be the compounding of my greatest problem?"

Fortunately, the answer is "Not necessarily." In the life of every manager who grasps for this seemingly plausible argument there can surely be found examples in practice which refute it. Consider one of the more likely situations—an assistant who is a stickler for detail and is now getting further and further behind in his work and missing critical deadlines. He is too close to the problem to sense that his passion for less consequential detail is now jeopardizing entire projects of far more serious consequence. He is behind ... but would you hesitate to advise him to *take time out* to analyze what he is doing? If need be, would you hesitate to take time out yourself to help him see the point? Of course you would not. The need for this prescription is usually painfully evident to all but the victim himself, who has become so immersed in the trees that all perspective of the forest has long since vanished.

True, if we, like Webster, could become vicariously convicted by the experience of others, it is conceivable that we could dispense with the inventorying of our time. We believe, and the great weight of expert opinion strongly supports the conviction, that the painful task of *changing our habits* will require far more conviction than is possible from the experience of others.

Only the amazing revelation that we are wasting great portions of the precious time entrusted to us ... that much of our effort is misdirected ... that many of the endeavors we seem unable to complete ought never to have been started ... only such painful experience can provide the determination to achieve the most difficult of all tasks—managing ourselves.

Not the least of the benefits to be gained from all of this

is the automatic correction tendency that sets in immediately. As the inventory discloses abuses of time, the remedies for which are self-evident, we find ourselves taking corrective action instinctively, without waiting for the procedure to run full course. Just as the supervisor, required for the first time to write out his own position description, discovers the greatest benefit in the thinking through of his job, so with the executive taking inventory of his time. Perhaps the greatest benefits of all lie in the initial discoveries.

Most people are not aware of what actually occupies their time. Yet it makes little sense to attempt to solve a problem without first assessing its nature and extent. And, as an early sage observed, a problem well stated is half solved. So with time. When we discover what we actually are doing with it, our task is half done.

Of the formats suggested for this critical inventory, *The Small Business Administration* makes available an excellent one prepared by Lee Chapman, director of Executive Time Studies, Inc.[3] This four-page study breaks down the normal working day into fifteen-minute segments, small enough for the precision required, large enough to avoid being unnecessarily detailed.

While the Chapman time study extends only from 9:00 A.M. to 4:45 P.M. we urge you to extend these times to your normal rising and retiring hours because of the importance of before- and after-work hours. On the sample chart shown on the following page arbitrary titles have been given to the six right-hand columns. These may or may not suit your particular convenience. They are, however, for planning and evaluation purposes. The critical columns for the inventory itself are the two left-hand columns titled "Planned" and "Actual." In the "Planned" column note the items you intend to accomplish during the day, at the approximate times you intend to accomplish them. In the "Actual" column record, at fifteen-minute intervals, what you actually did. One or two words should suffice for each entry. Examples might be shown: "10 letters;" or "D-Brown, Hatch, Miller" (D=dictate); or "C-Rose, Thornton" (C=call); or "Comm. Mtg."; or "L-Harrison" (L=lunch).

Other headings which might be useful would be "Promotion," "Reading," or "Talking" (Telephone, Personal, or Meeting).

Planned	Time	Actual	Inside Office	Indirect Outside	Un-Accountable	Admin.	Planning	Other
	7:00							
	7:15							
	7:30							
	7:45							
	8:00							
	8:15							
	8:30							
	8:45							
	9:00							
	9:15							
	9:30							
	9:45							
	10:00							
	10:15							
	10:30							
	10:45							
	11:00							
	11:15							
	11:30							
	11:45							
	12:00							
	12:15							
	12:30							
	12:45							
	1:00							
	1:15							
	1:30							
	1:45							
	2:00							
	2:15							
	2:30							
	2:45							
	3:00							
	3:15							
	3:30							
	3:45							
	4:00							
	4:15							
	4:30							
	4:45							
	5:00							
	5:15							
	5:30							
	5:45							
	6:00							
	6:15							
	6:30							
	6:45							
	7:00							
	7:15							
	7:30							
	7:45							
	8:00							
	8:15							
	8:30							
	8:45							
	9:00							
	9:15							
	9:30							
	9:45							
	10:00							

What we are doing to find out where the time goes is simply to list the different things we do, as we do them. The duration for this inventory is generally suggested to be from two to three months. The cyclical nature of your work may affect this decision.

When your time inventory for the week has been completed, it is essential that you *classify the results* in the manner that will be most useful to your own particular requirements. Thus the headings for the six right-hand columns should be selected for purposes of useful analysis rather than ease of inventory. Dr. Joseph Trickett, Professor of Management at the Santa Clara College of Business Administration, recommends a useful division into four "Activity Analysis Sheets."[4] These provide the benefit of allowing you to group and rearrange the things you must do in terms of their relative importance and urgency. By thus listing the items separately, you can avoid the powerful tendency to confuse the *urgent* with the *important*.

The higher the executive rises, the greater becomes his problem of having adequate time, and the more he is forced to confine his activities to the really important and the genuinely urgent. As General Eisenhower arranged his affairs so that only the truly important and urgent matters came across his desk, he discovered that the two seldom went together. He found that the really important matters were seldom urgent . . . and that the most urgent matters were seldom important.

This discovery has a most interesting application in the area of assumed procrastination. While we are told not to put off until tomorrow what can be done today, the conclusion that the urgent matters clamoring for immediate attention are seldom the most important introduces an element of caution well worth considering. The counter-admonition thus would read: "Do *not* do today what can be put off until tomorrow." The Christian executive who first called this factor to the authors' attention has been so impressed with the effectiveness of deliberate postponement, under appropriate circumstances of course, that he tries always to ask the question, "Would this situation benefit by deliberate delay?"

Behind this intriguing reversal of usual advice lies the well-founded assumption that an analysis of tasks facing the modern executive will reveal plenty of jobs which *do* require attention *today*, and are of sufficient import to warrant immediate action. Further, it may be assumed that some of the less important (though seemingly urgent) matters will actually *disappear* with postponement. So the one Christian executive reported his experience to be. What more efficient disposition of overburdening tasks could ever be devised! The discerning executive need not be cautioned against excessive or injudicious application of this principle!

Dr. Trickett suggests heading the four "Activity Analysis Sheets" as follows: (1) "Intrinsic Importance"; (2) "Urgency"; (3) "Delegation"; and (4) "Visitations and Conferences." The sheets, with appropriate subheadings, would appear as on the following page.

In the process of transferring activities to these four activity sheets, significant perspective will be gained. The most urgent tasks are separated from the least urgent; the most important from the least important; the conferences and conferees most frequently required from those least frequently required. Under the "Delegation" heading, the names of any subordinates or associates capable of assuming delegated tasks will be listed and appropriate tasks assigned under columns.

At this point make a list of "Ideal Activities" which ought to occupy your time. Theoretically this should be a summary of those items in the left-hand columns of each of the analysis sheets. In addition, of course, you must consider any items from your revised position description whose importance warrants inclusion, even though you may not have done any work on them because of lack of time.

We have now answered the question posed at the outset of this chapter: "Where has the time gone?" We have taken inventory of most, if not all, of the "sixty golden minutes" of each hour and have attempted to answer the critical question "What results have I actually accomplished?" We have already experienced the built-in tendency to apply corrective action even while the process of discovery was going on.

Pick Your Best Strategy

We dare not leave to chance alone the effective utilization of our time. Having tested our resources (by personal inventory) ... reviewed our opportunities (by job inventory) ... and learned where our time goes (by time

ACTIVITY ANALYSIS
1. Intrinsic Importance

VERY IMPORTANT	IMPORTANT	NOT SO IMPORTANT	UNIMPORTANT
Absolutely must be done.	Should be done.	May not be necessary, but may be useful.	Can be eliminated entirely.

ACTIVITY ANALYSIS
2. Urgency

VERY URGENT	URGENT	NOT URGENT	TIME NOT A FACTOR
Must be done NOW.	Should be done soon. Short-term.	Long-range.	

ACTIVITY ANALYSIS
3. Delegation

MUST BE DONE BY ME.	CAN BE DELEGATED TO (A)	CAN BE DELEGATED OR ASSIGNED TO (B)	CAN BE DELEGATED OR ASSIGNED TO (C)	CAN BE DELEGATED OR ASSIGNED TO (D)
I am only person who can do.				

ACTIVITY ANALYSIS
4. Visitations and Conferences

PEOPLE I MUST SEE EACH DAY	PEOPLE TO SEE FREQUENTLY: NOT DAILY	PEOPLE TO SEE REGULARLY: NOT FREQUENTLY	PEOPLE TO SEE ONLY INFREQUENTLY	OTHER PERSONAL CONTACTS

inventory) ... we come now to the strategic problem of
how best to apply our resources to our opportunities for
optimum results.

Webster defines "strategy" as the science and art of
employing resources to achieve objectives. We must therefore be certain of our objectives. Both organizational and
personal objectives become involved at this point. There
are those who hold that it is impossible for both an
organization and its key individuals to achieve their objectives. Dissatisfaction, they argue, is inevitable for one or
the other. Charles Hughes, industrial psychologist with
Texas Instruments, believes otherwise,[5] and strongly recommends that management (1) break down company
objectives into subgoals stated in terms meaningful to people at lower levels; (2) communicate goals to all employees; (3) work through supervisors to help individual
employees set their own goals; (4) allow for some modification of tentative organizational objectives; and (5) recom-
bine and redefine organizational and personal objectives
until a balance is reached between them.

Hughes does not suggest that organizational objectives
be subordinated to employees' goals. His point is that the
employees and the organizations must be willing and able
to adapt their aims to each other's needs.

Having thus clarified our objectives, and having analyzed all of the tasks facing us as we pursue these
objectives, we see the imperative of concentrating on the
essentials. The first step of our strategic plan emerges as
the need to confine our efforts to the essential tasks—
"essential" meaning those which cannot be delegated or
postponed.

We have also reviewed the concept of becoming "opportunity-oriented" rather than "problem-oriented." William Oncken crystallizes this concept by comparing managers who spend their time (a) refining yesterday's solutions to last year's problems; (b) fighting fires—striving
today for results that were expected yesterday; or (c)
taking action today to get results tomorrow, that were
planned yesterday.

There appears to be a vicious cycle for the "problem-
oriented" manager. The more he worries about problems,
the more problems arise to worry about. The more he
concentrates on remedying mistakes of the past, the less he
has time to plan to meet the needs of tomorrow, which

thus continue to become mistakes because they weren't anticipated. The obvious solution appears to lie in organization of time to plan ahead, which will be discussed more thoroughly in the next chapter. Suffice it to say here that the more a manager can delegate the routine matters which consume his time, and the more effectively he can apply that "saved" time to projecting ahead, the fewer problems there will be *and* the greater the probability of capitalizing on opportunities. The second concept of our strategy therefore is to concentrate on our opportunities, not our problems. If we let them, and many of us do, problems could absorb *all* of our effort. By real effort, our energies and resources must be redirected to maximizing our opportunities so that we become, in a very real sense, "opportunity-oriented."

A third principle of strategy is, while redirecting your efforts toward opportunities rather than problems, also to think creatively about new opportunities which may never have been identified. This may be a difficult endeavor, particularly for those who have been immersed in their problems for so long that creative thinking has ceased. In industry many variations of this can be observed in such exercises as "brainstorming." A great emphasis on the value of creative thinking is seen in many aspects of industrial management today. As new opportunities are sought, your organizational objectives and particular resources must be kept in mind. It is those particular opportunities which are peculiarly fitted . . . or which *may* be *made* peculiarly fitted . . . to your objectives and resources, that will be of interest.

Finally, as a fourth possible concept for your strategy, of all the possible courses of action or combinations thereof, which one best suits the objectives you seek . . . best utilizes your available and anticipated resources . . . best capitalizes your present and potential opportunities . . . gives maximum results for effort and materials expended? This should be your strategy.

Work Your Plan

The eighteenth-century Scottish poet Robert Burns has often been quoted to the effect that even the best-laid plans can go astray. Planning your work, then, is not enough. You must work your plan!

Lest you take this assignment lightly, consider the

powerful factors at work opposing its successful execution. Working your plans means cutting out nonessential tasks; it means delegating to others; it means majoring in planning ahead instead of repairing the dikes—in short, it means changing your ways as a manager. This can be the toughest job you've ever faced.

Imagine at the outset that you are examining with a magnifying glass the things you've done on a given day and are asking the questions "Was this trip necessary? Did this job really need to be done? Could it have been done better or as well by someone else? Could it have been postponed? Did I sense a divine commission in the doing of it? Did I do it because I like doing those things . . . because that's the department I used to be in myself, and, after all, I know that field pretty well?" These can be exceedingly uncomfortable questions . . . and honest answers can come hard.

Confining your efforts only to the essential can mean no longer saving for the right time those things you really like to do. . . . Those things generally are least essential! Delegating to others can be most difficult. Fear that the job won't be done as well . . . fear that it may be done better . . . doubts about the appearance of a job that is shrinking rather than growing . . . all can make delegation difficult.

Problems may be distasteful, but in this area there is substance and generally a body of known or discoverable facts with which to work. This can be much more gratifying than planning into the future where conditions must be projected and broad conclusions based on mere assumptions. Instead of a structured situation, this poses ambiguities which can be disconcerting to one who favors working in the former situation.

Thus the matter of "working your plan" may be more easily said than done. Implementation presents a barrier for many managers. Some prefer not to move *until the plan is complete in all detail.* In areas of advance planning this is not always possible. For others the *fear of failure* hangs over implementation of any plan. Called by many authors the "greatest enemy of management," this fear must be faced. The atmosphere set by top management can increase or reduce this fear . . . but it is likely to be present to some extent in almost every managerial situation.

Failure, treated constructively, can be viewed as one of

the greatest learning tools available to management. No one questions that we learn much more quickly and lastingly from our mistakes than our successes. (But don't be guilty of making the same mistake twice!) No one denies that virtually all of the great discoveries of history were preceded by failures. Yet we permit the fear of failure to stunt the growth of our executives . . . to hang like a pall over our organizations . . . to quench the spirit of innovation and experimentation so essential to growth and new discovery. If we agree that the ability to benefit from failure can lead to heightened effectiveness, then failure loses its stigma. We can view it more objectively and constructively.

Managers who require performance appraisals and interviews that include regular discussion of failures along with successes find that it *is* possible to deal constructively with the problem. Getting it on the table for discussion in a routine, casual way does a great deal to ease the tension which otherwise surrounds the subject. Management is encouraged to let its people know that without mistakes little progress can be expected . . . that it prefers to see calm lessons learned from mistakes rather than panic-action to prevent future mistakes. A healthy philosophy of mistakes could improve the likelihood of successful implementation of your plan.

It is said of delegation that along with the right to decide must be delegated the "right to be wrong." When a subordinate makes a mistake and is called on the carpet without real consideration of all the factors—including the responsibility of those who should have assisted and supported and ensured complete understanding from the top —such a subordinate is not likely to accept the next delegated assignment with as much enthusiasm. One of the cardinal errors in delegation is taking back the job when something goes wrong, instead of assisting in determining what's going wrong, why, and what can be done about it. The act of taking back the job destroys the relationship of confidence which must exist for delegation to be successful. Instead of taking back the task, the one who delegated should be asking himself where he failed in carrying out the responsibilities of delegation which lie most heavily on the person doing the delegation.

As with the setting of goals, care should be taken to make the undertaking realistic and achievable. Better to start off bite-size than never to start because of the size of the task. The most important part of any journey, however, long or short, is taking the first step.

REFERENCES

[1]—Webster, Eric, "Need More Time?", *Supervisory Management,* January, 1964.

[2]—Webster, Eric, "Let's Repeal Parkinson's Law," *Management Review,* American Management Association, October, 1962.

[3]—Chapman, Lee Patrick, "Surveying and Controlling Executive Time," *The Small Business Administration,* No. 76.

[4]—Trickett, Dr. Joseph M., "A More Effective Use of Time," *California Management Review,* Summer, 1962.

[5]—Hughes, Charles, *The Manager's Letter,* American Management Association, October 20, 1965.

CHAPTER 7

WHAT IS YOUR PROGRESS?
—ARE YOU IMPROVING?

An organization can give a man the title of manager, but only the man can make himself into one.

—Joseph Mason

JAMES BLACK presents in his book[1] a perceptive discussion of the "Road to Self-Improvement." In recounting an incident at a certain training seminar, he struck what must have been a chord of response in every reader who had ever attended such a seminar. The problem being discussed was "how to sell top management" on their programs. One member of the group remarked heatedly, "The trouble is that high-level executives give only lip service to training. They want it because they think they should have it, but they don't want to be bothered with the details. They are not really interested in training. They resist new ideas." This struck a real spark. Immediately other conferees began to relate experiences of their own in which they had been rebuffed by their superiors when they sought to introduce improved methods or different ways of doing things. One said, "The truth is that the wrong people are at this meeting. Our bosses should be here."

An older man was sitting at the end of the table. He had said little throughout the seminar, but had listened attentively. The identifying badge he wore on his coat lapel gave only his name and company. He was simply a member of the group, and a silent one at that. But now he had something to say.

"I think you fellows are being very hard on top management. I find most executives are receptive to new ideas if y are good. They have to be. But men who have the final decision in management are cautious. They cannot afford to go off half-cocked. Therefore, when you make recommendations to them you must be sure they are well thought out and that they are useful to the company as a whole. Perhaps it is not top management that is rigid in its views. Perhaps it is we in the training field. Perhaps our problem is that we are interested only in training as such. We make no special effort to learn the other functions of management. If we had a comprehensive understanding of all of the problems of a company, maybe we would be better training men."

After this observation the older man sat back in his chair and for the remainder of the meeting listened silently as the discussion moved to other subjects. At the end of the seminar the association manager said to him, "I hope you found this interesting. You should have let me tell the group who you are."

"No," was the reply, "I prefer to attend meetings of this kind quietly. It is up to me to know the latest developments in every area of management. If those men had realized I was president of my company, they might not have talked so freely. Certainly they would never have taken me into the group on equal terms. After all, I come to these meetings to learn something, not to express my views."

Here was the president of a large Tennessee textile mill who had a *planned program of attendance at seminars and courses* in every phase of management. On his staff he had experts who were capable of administering the details of the various operations of his company, but he believed he could give his subordinates more effective direction if he familiarized himself with their specialties.

An estimated 750,000 supervisors, managers and executives are annually attending conferences and seminars on management problems, convincing evidence that the awareness of the importance of this critical tool is spreading rapidly. The rate at which new developments are occurring in managerial fields accentuates the urgency of the course of action for those who wish to sharpen their managerial skills. Continuing education for management men must be made a part of the job. It must be a mainstream activity, not merely something for nights and week ends.

One Christian executive was asked how he had benefited from the management seminar he had attended. After a moment's reflection he said that the results, only six months after the conference, could be seen throughout his organization, particularly in his keymen. Two principles emphasized in the seminar had proved applicable to a number of situations in the work, both in the United States and abroad. The first principle was that it is more important to have right questions, when facing a problem, than to have right answers. "Right answers," arrived at hastily, may prove to be short-lived and unrealistic. Often they are "guesses" which seem appropriate at the moment but may be unrelated to the *real* problem. The right questions aim to uncover facts; ascertain the *real* problem; determine probable cause or causes; generate alternative solutions; and select the best course of remedial action.

The second principle which had proved useful was "management by objectives." Put in the form of questions, the principle appears as follows: What are your objectives? What are your resources? What are your opportunities? What is your strategy for applying resources to opportunities for maximum progress toward your objectives?

Upon returning home from a seminar to which he took one of his key assistants,[2] this same executive, to whom we referred earlier, was asked how relevant such a seminar, designed for industrial executives, was to the needs of his Christian organization. He replied enthusiastically that he judged it to be eighty per cent applicable and tremendously worth while over-all.

Managers and executives in Christian organizations should appreciate management as a profession, approach it with respect, and determine to master it.

The *building of a management library* is important. Just as exposure to other managers, as in seminars, conferences and courses, is a refreshing, stimulating and provocative experience, so exposure to the literature of management is vital to one who would manage. "A management library," according to Auren Uris, editor of the Management Development Division of the Research Institute of America, "is becoming just as important for the professional executive as the technical library is for the engineer. Behind the academic activity lies a basic idea: management is a profession that can be taught and learned."[3] While most bibliographies are discouragingly long, any effort to present a few of the best selections invites criticism for the omissions. Nonetheless, conviction of the importance of this beginning for the reader who may not have begun a serious study of the profession of management impels the recommendation of a few of the better-known works, including some of a highly practical value (see "Recommended Management Publications" p. 75 ff.):

Subscription to at least one of the top *management periodicals* is recommended. Several excellent publications come with the personal membership in the American Management Association. Particularly for the chief executives in Christian organizations, this membership is highly recommended.

Membership in professional organizations provides contact with other executives with similar problems and responsibilities. Occasional meetings of such associations provide the manager with a break in the routine; a chance to "get perspective" on his job; an occasion to mix with others who have faced similar problems and may provide valuable answers; and an opportunity to hear professionals present a field or area of management of interest.

One of the hazards of management is the tendency of executives to view their organization from the perspective of a specialist. It is not surprising that a person whose training and experience has been in personnel, for example, should tend to view organizational matters through personnel-oriented eyes. Nor is it surprising that he tends to continue to operate in this area, even making decisions which, in all other departments, would be left to the department manager.

Many executives, when first confronted with this tendency, immediately recognize the description of their own activities. From this realization has come the *concept of the "generalist"* as the man who is needed for modern management. He is a man who not only can make the necessary adjustment to the managerial view of the overall organization . . . he also realizes that the rapidly developing techniques and specialties in the field of management require that the man at the top have an over-all grasp of objectives, resources, opportunities and strategy but that the technical knowledge required for departmental operations should be left to specialists within the organization. The modern manager has his hands full mastering the profession of management. Let him, whenever possible, stay with that.

A *questioning mind* has been suggested by many as an essential chracteristic of the manager. Such a mind is alert to change; is constantly in quest of facts; relates facts to situations and projects them into future possibilities; views interruptions as opportunities; seeks relationships between facts, situations and people; contemplates strategy.

The *importance of preparation* has been emphasized as the most important single factor in turning opportunity into success. Preparation required for your own job should be evident from a review of your position description ... or its development, if none exists. For any manager other than the chief executive, the position description of his superior, or another in a position to which he aspires, presents valid requirements for preparation. There is no better candidate for advancement than the person who, while handling his own job in an exemplary fashion, has also prepared himself for the job above. Meanwhile, there is no better assistant than one who understands the job, comprehends relationships, and is sensitive to the situational environment.

In the area of self-development, the question may be raised concerning the quest for excellence. Is it Christian to aspire to a position of leadership? Without becoming unnecessarily involved with theological issues, the writers are of the conviction that responsible stewardship of one's talents may require no less. The nurture and development of the gifts God has given to each of us must surely be acknowledged as a requisite to returning to Him our best. For a Christian, with talents leading to managerial responsibilities, aspirations to excellence in his performance and opportunity for maximum service to his Lord would appear imperative. So *set your goals high* and strive for excellence. Cultivate a "passion for excellence." In the final chapter this is presented as the Christian standard.

"If we ask what our society inspires in the way of high performance," warns the Rockefeller Brothers Fund report, "we are led to the conclusion that we may have, to a startling degree, lost the gift for demanding high performance of ourselves."[4] Emerson said our chief want in life is for someone who will make us do what we can. The former president of the Carnegie Foundation, John

Gardner, stated, "The idea for which this nation stands will not survive if the highest goal free men can set themselves is an amiable mediocrity.... But excellence implies more than competence. It implies a striving for the highest standards in every phase of life. We need individual excellence in all its forms—in every kind of creative endeavor, in political life, in education, in industry—in short, universally."[5]

The *implications of change* in organizations . . . its management . . . and winning acceptance of it from your people . . . have assumed major proportions for the modern manager. While this may be considered as but one of the many managerial concepts, it has far-reaching consequences in areas such as standards of performance, accommodations to problems of growth, and management development. In a later work John Gardner reminds us of the "mind-forged manacles" which our aging society and organizations have developed as defenses against new ideas.[6] Broad-mindedness . . . appreciation of innovation . . . stimulation of creativity . . . all have their rightful place in the portfolio of the modern manager.

What *kinds of knowledge* are important to executives? David Ewing presents one of the most useful answers to this question, electing to use the term "level" in describing each category.[7] The *first* level of importance is methods or techniques, a good example of which is one's problem-analysis of decision-making method or technique. The importance of this technique to successful management is obvious.

The *second* level of knowledge important to the manager is information about his environment—the realities of the situation surrounding the organization and the manager. This would involve people or conditions or trends perhaps. A fund-raising drive typifies a problem-solving situation requiring efforts to collect knowledge relating to the time that prospective donors are likely to be in a receptive frame of mind, undistracted by tax deadlines, other fund drives, or adverse publicity. The factor of judgment enters at this point, making it a more difficult area in which to test capabilities than the area of problem-solving.

The *third* level of knowledge has to do with what managers want to happen, conditions they desire, goals they seek. Analytical thinking plays a supporting role to insight, imagination and vision. This area may be more "intuitional" than "factual" in nature. An executive, feeling that the climate of supervision in his department is too rigid ... too authoritarian ... decides to relax the rules and to allow more freedom. This decision resulted from reading about patterns of supervision and observing and talking with people in his department about conditions. Intelligence and related tests are not useful in evaluating facility with knowledge at this level. Intuition and performance records are more useful as guides here.

At this point our respect for the requirements placed upon the managerial mind as compared with those placed upon the minds of those in other professions and vocations has risen considerably. We can conclude, with Ewing, that administrative requirements for knowledge are not limited to any single type of information, at least three levels of knowledge being involved; that capacity to deal with different levels of knowledge may vary greatly among equally intelligent people—and may vary greatly during a single career; that the quality of executive judgment is related to facility with knowledge at the various levels; that the ability to persuade is more important in relation to knowledge at the third level (goals) than at the first (problem-solving); and, finally, a man advancing in management should find value in kinds of preparation other than formal training programs (through reading, informal talks and reflection).

Auren Uris suggests the following checklist for the executive who wants to keep abreast of change in the management profession:[8]

1. In your industry have you increased your contacts by—
   a. Reading the journals in your field?
   b. Increasing your participation in a professional group or association of men who do similar work?
   c. Attending conferences and lectures, or interviewing experts, to keep up with changes in your industry [author's note—in Christian organizational activity]?
2. Inside your organization have you shown signs of personal growth by—
   a. Talking shop regularly with your colleagues?
   b. Making changes in your way of handling assignments?
   c. Taking on new assignments?
3. In your quest for job knowledge have you—

   a. Visited other companies that are now working on problems you may soon be encountering?

   b. Kept up with the stream of ideas available in current management literature—for example, *Harvard Business Review, Fortune, Dun's Review* and *Modern Industry?*

   c. Investigated what's available at local schools?

   d. Made suggestions, either to a top company executive or to schools, for studies of interest to you?

4. In pursuit of your professional interests have you—

   a. Experimented in the application of new methods to executive problems?

   b. Experimented in the development of new methods to complete your daily tasks?

   c. Tried as much as possible to substitute method and system for casualness and the impromptu solution?

   d. Kept in touch with the kind of thinking going on at Arden House, Harvard Business School, the University of Chicago's Management Development Program, and so on?

In one sense this entire book is about self-development. In this chapter special emphasis has been given to a few concepts which warrant attention. No two management consultants would be in complete agreement on any given management development program for an individual. They would agree that the person who can help the manager most is . . . himself.

REFERENCES

[1]—Black, James Menzies, *Assignment: Management,* Prentice-Hall, New Jersey, 1961.

[2]—Seminar on "Finance for the Non-financial Executive," Management Institute, University of Wisconsin, Madison, Wisconsin.

[3]—*Op. cit.*

[4]—"The Pursuit of Excellence," *America at Mid-Century Series,* Rockefeller Brothers Fund, Inc., 1958.

[5]—Gardner, John W., *Excellence,* Harper and Brothers, New York, 1961.

[6]—Gardner, John W., *Self-Renewal,* Harper and Row, New York, 1964.

[7]—Ewing, David W., *The Managerial Mind,* the Free Press, New York, 1964.

[8]—*Op. cit.*

Recommended Management Publications Exhibit A

Administrative Science Quarterly, Graduate School of Business and Public Administration, Cornell University, Ithaca, New York.

Advanced Management Journal, Society for the Advancement of Management, 16 West 40th Street, New York 10018.

Business Horizons, Graduate School of Business, Indiana University, Bloomington, Indiana.

Business Management, the Management Publishing Group, Inc., 22 West Putnam Avenue, Greenwich, Connecticut 06830.

California Management Review, Graduate School of Business Administration, University of California, Los Angeles, California.

Harvard Business Review, Graduate School of Business Administration, Harvard University, Cambridge, Massachusetts.

American Management Association Exhibit B

The A.M.A. has 35,000 members in a hundred countries of the world. An individual membership of sixty dollars annually provides membership in two divisions—one major and one of supplementary interest (i.e., General Management and Personnel). Four regular periodicals are included with membership: *The Management Review*, on a monthly basis, digests and abstracts the best in current business reading; *Personnel*, a bimonthly magazine covering all phases of the personnel function from selection and appraisal to communication and wage administration; *Management News*, a monthly summary of A.M.A. activities featuring "The President's Scratchpad," commenting on timely management patterns, and "The Listening Post," reviewing current management problems and developments; and *The Manager's Letter*, providing concise information on new management ideas, practices and trends.

Management reports, *management bulletins* and *research studies* on all phases of management are regularly issued to the individual member according to his divisional memberships. He is also entitled to full use of the *management information service*, in which a trained staff backed with excellent library facilities will research any management problem with which they come into contact.

The A.M.A.'s outstanding *management film library* of more than a hundred films is available to members on a reduced rental basis. *Special publications,* including many books on management, are available at reduced rate.

Seminars, courses and conferences—more than a thousand of them each year—are offered to members at reduced rates. Subjects range all the way from "management courses" of four weeks (split up) to "developing leadership skills," and from "office management" to "finance."

Associations   Exhibit C

American Management Association
135 West 50th Street, New York, New York 10020

American Institute of Management
125 West 38th Street, New York, New York 10016

Association for Public Relations Council
National Association of Church Business Managers
National Association of Purchasing Agents
Society for Advancement of Management
16 West 40th Street, New York, New York 10018

Seminars, Institutes and Conferences   Exhibit D

American Management Association
135 West 50th Street, New York, New York 10020
(Write for catalog.)

Management Institute, University of Wisconsin
Madison, Wisconsin (Write for catalog.)

Colleges and universities (Write for catalog of evening
courses and executive development seminars.)

Christian Stewardship Council (Annual Session)
Evon Hedley, c/o CBMCI, Glen Ellyn, Illinois

Committee on Annuities (Annual Conference on Voluntary Giving)
450 Park Avenue, New York, New York 10022

Seminar on Estate Planning (Dr. Carleton Ponsford)
Pasadena College, Pasadena, California

L.S.U. Seminar on Taxes, Estate Planning and Charitable Giving
c/o Robert Sharpe, P.O. 17062, Memphis, Tennessee 38117

National Conference on Solicitations (National Council on Philanthropy)

Furlough Missionary Leadership Conference
America's Keswick, Whiting, New Jersey

Louis A. Allen Management Seminar (Louis A. Allen and Associates)
526 Forest Avenue, Palo Alto, California 94301

* Recommendations for a half-dozen selections with which to start your "Basic Management Bookshelf."

* Allen, Louis A., *The Management Profession*, McGraw-Hill, New York, 1964. (Lists four basic functions, nineteen activities and numerous principles of management. Discusses each understandably and with illustrations.)

* Appley, Lawrence A., *Management in Action*, American Management Association, New York, 1956. (The basic collection of writings of the current president of the American Management Association. Touches leadership, communication, management responsibility, employee morale and executive appraisal.)

_____, *The Management Evolution*, American Management Association, New York, 1963. (Emphasizes new developments in profession of management and practical ways to "make things happen." Includes determining long- and short-range objectives; assigning responsibility effectively; developing and motivating people; keeping an organization dynamic, dissatisfied with status quo.)

Barnard, Chester I., *The Functions of the Executive*, Harvard University Press, Cambridge, 1964. (A revision and expansion of lectures at Lowell Institute in Boston in 1937 by the author, formerly president of the New Jersey Bell Telephone Company and of the Rockefeller Foundation. Treats the theory of authority, environment of decision, the executive process and executive responsibility.)

Bennett, C. L., *Defining the Manager's Job*, American Management Association, New York, 1958. (*The A.M.A. Manual of Position Descriptions*. Reproduces 150 actual position descriptions based on an A.M.A. survey of 140 companies at all managerial levels. Includes useful information on how descriptions are prepared and the uses to which they may be put.)

Black, James Menzies, *Assignment: Management*, Prentice-Hall, Englewood Cliffs, New Jersey, 1961. (A "guide to constructive self-appraisal for managers." Treats characteristics of command; organization—foundation of efficiency; planning—key to management success; leadership.)

_____, *Developing Competent Subordinates*, American Management Association, New York, 1961. (The author, formerly manager of the A.M.A.'s Personnel Division, presents in practical fashion the tools of management development with special emphasis on selection; on-the-job training; delegation; job rotation; and counseling. An A.M.A. handbook.)

Doris, Lillian, and Miller, Besse May, *Complete Secretary's Handbook*, Prentice-Hall, Englewood Cliffs, New Jersey, 1960. ("An entire office library in one handy volume." Thorough development of techniques for usual secretarial duties [from handling callers to arranging travel]; writing good letters; writing correctly [from grammar to capitalization]; employer's personal work [from social amenities to personal taxes]; employer's financial affairs; and advanced secretarial techniques [from preparing legal papers to acting as corporate secretary]. Every effective manager who has a secretary needs an efficient one. To be efficient, a secretary needs a good handbook for fast, accurate answers.)

° Drucker, Peter F., *The Practice of Management*, Harper and Brothers, New York, 1954. (Selecting this as a "Blue Ribbon" book, Harper's called it "the most authoritative, penetrating analysis yet made of business management." The author, a leading corporation consultant, analyzes the nature of management [its role, its jobs and its challenge]; management and development of managers; the Chief Executive and the Board; the structure of management; the management of worker and of work; and what it means to be a manager.)

Dubin, Robert, *Human Relations in Administration*, Prentice-Hall, Inc., Englewood Cliffs, New Jersey, 1961. (Research Professor in the University of Oregon's Department of Sociology. Presents well-chosen selection of numerous papers systematically organized around key concepts such as Bureaucracy; Executives; Specialists; Power; Authority; Communications; Decision-Making; Leadership; and Control.)

Ewing, David W., *The Managerial Mind,* the Free Press, New York, 1964. (An associate editor of *Harvard Business Review,* the author deals first with the intellectual characteristics which distinguish the manager's approach to problems; then such interesting subjects as nonconformity; the value of tension; attitude toward manipulation; tolerance for waste and inefficiency; levels of knowledge in managerial thinking; teaching and the managerial mind; and the element of creativity in management.)

Heyel, Carl, *Organizing Your Job in Management,* American Management Association, New York, 1960. (An A.M.A. handbook selected primarily for its emphasis on the management of time through effective organization of work, of subordinates' assignments, and future planning. Suggests ways to direct tensions into productive channels, analyze your work habits, get the most out of meetings, and delegate assignments effectively. Includes practical suggestions for organizing yourself, your desk, and your department.)

Houle, Cyril O., *The Effective Board,* Association Press, New York, 1960. (Dr. Houle, Professor of Education at the University of Chicago, has directed Board-member training institutes co-sponsored by the University and the Welfare Council of Metropolitan Chicago. The author traces the needs for Boards, how they developed, and their infinite variety. Also discussed are selection of Board members; orienting and inducting them; organization of the Board; responsibilities of the Board; Board-executive-staff relationships; suggestions for improving the Board's effectiveness; and a rating scale for measuring your Board.)

Howe, Reuel L., *The Miracle of Dialogue,* the Seabury Press, New York, 1963. (A penetrating, discerning analysis of the critical area of communication from the Christian perspective. Describes dialogue, the principle of communication, as the act by which individuals and groups make themselves available to and become aware of each other. A careful look at pitfalls such as overpersuasiveness, over-specific counseling, and glossing-over of opposing views.)

Hughes, Charles L., *Goal-Setting—Key to Individual and Organizational Effectiveness,* American Management Association, New York, 1965. (New emphasis is placed on the importance of both organizational and personal goals to the effective performance, survival and growth of organizations. Discusses need for recognizing requirements of self-fulfillment and job satisfaction, stimulation of goal-seeking behavior, and the making of "management by results" a reality. Need to harmonize individual and organizational goals is stressed. Describes how to break down overall objectives into subgoals that managers and employees at all levels can grasp, associate themselves with and contribute toward achieving, thus creating both individual and organization success.)

Jennings, Eugene E., *The Executive*, Harper and Row, New York, 1963. (Describing the essential characteristics of the executive's role, Dr. Jennings, Professor of Business Administration at Michigan State's Graduate School of Business Administration, portrays three common executive styles . . . autocratic, democratic and bureaucratic. The problem facing modern executives is not to choose which of the three is best, for few executives can or should be exclusively one or the other. The problem is which of the ingredients to select from each for your most effective style. Modern managers are advised to "pick your leadership pattern." This book will help you begin. See also the author's *Anatomy of Leadership*, which concludes that our society's chief characteristic is a lost sense of self-direction evidenced by the tendency to escape from leadership responsibility.)

Kahn, Robert L., and Boulding, Elise, *Power and Conflict in Organizations*, Basic Books, Inc., New York, 1964. (Sponsored by the Foundation for Research on Human Behavior, Ann Arbor, this work represents contributions from nine leading social scientists and more than fifty corporation executives participating in seminars of the Foundation. Examines principles of conflict and responses to situations of competition and conflict. Their aim: to find ways in which a leader can exercise power without creating conflict that wastes organizational energies and damages individuals. Kahn is Associate Professor of Psychology and Program Director, Survey Research Center, University of Michigan.)

Kellogg, Marion S., *What to Do About Performance Appraisal*, American Management Association, New York, 1965. (An A.M.A. handbook selected by its Presidents'

Association because of its excellent handling of this most demanding of the executive skills. Appraisal is essential to promote or fire, counsel or criticize, coach or transfer. A practical "how-to-do-it" book with many pluses.)

Likert, Rensis, *New Patterns of Management*, McGraw-Hill, New York, 1961. (Dr. Likert, co-founder of the Institute for Social Research, an interdisciplinary center for research on practical and theoretical problems relating to leadership, organizational performance, improvement and change, economic motivation and behavior, and communication and influence. The work, a triple-award winner in the year of its publication, reflects the author's keen interest in managerial theory and practice. Proposes a new management system utilizing such procedures as budgets, goals and work simplification, but with a different set of motivational principles promising better results with appreciably fewer resentments, hostilities, grievances and breakdowns inherent in the present system. Discusses new variables and measurements for decision-making guides. While devoted to study of business enterprise, material is equally applicable to government, hospital, educational and voluntary institutions.)

* McGregor, Douglas, *The Human Side of Enterprise*, McGraw-Hill, New York, 1960. (The author, past president of Antioch College and now Professor of Management at M.I.T.'s School of Industrial Management, developed the famous "suppositions"—*Theory X*—the assumptions upon which traditional organizations are based now appearing inadequate for full utilization of human potentialities—and *Theory Y*— the assumptions consistent with current research knowledge which could lead to higher motivation and greater realization of both individual and organizational goals.

McQuaig, Jack H., *How to Pick Men*, Frederick Fell, Inc., New York, 1963. (The author, head of the McQuaig Institute of Executive Training, holds that no organization can be better than the men who work for it—thus executive selection is a critical management skill. Deals with how to appraise men; specific questions to ask job applicants; interpretation of facts elicited; and how to determine capacity for leadership and responsibility.

* Mandell, Milton M., *The Selection Process*, American Management Association, New York, 1964. (The author, for seventeen years Chief of Management Selection Methods for the United States Civil Service Commission, is currently Personnel Consultant to the Internal Revenue Service. Choosing the right man for the right job can be the manager's most difficult decision—and this decision is made nine million times a year. The cost of finding, screening, testing, placing, orienting and training a new employee is rising steadily. The techniques necessary for an effective selection program are becoming increasingly numerous and complex. As an aid in personnel management, this work discusses methods of selection, recruiting, reference checking and interviewing—at all levels.)

Miner, John B., *The Management of Ineffective Performance,* McGraw-Hill, New York, 1963. (Dr. Miner, Professor of Management in the School of Business Administration, University of Oregon, provides a new insight and a fresh approach to the important problem of what to do about unacceptable performance. Factual data on ineffective performance is followed by theoretical background on each area, its influence on performance, and remedies.)

Rowland, Virgil K., *Managerial Performance Standards,* American Management Association, New York, 1960. (An A.M.A. Fellow in executive development, the author is assistant to the president of the Detroit Edison Company. He believes that setting managerial performance standards is one of management's most valuable techniques. Recognized and widely used on tangible production factors such as quality, quantity and costs, the same techniques are applicable to and badly needed for the intangibles of management. The process of superior and subordinate working together to establish and realize workable and meaningful standards itself makes a great contribution to organizational success.)

* Schleh, Edward C., *Management by Results,* McGraw-Hill, New York, 1961. (President of Schleh Associates, management consultants, the author is an award-winning contributor to management thinking. Having counseled "results-oriented" management for twenty years, he now sees his basic principles being widely adopted in industry. Deals with objectives; individual initiative; accountability. Shows why the function of a records system must be to stimulate sound management action. Benefits include sounder decision-making at all levels; closer understanding

of direction between executives and subordinates; motivates greater individual achievement; and develops long-range perspective.)

Uris, Auren, *The Efficient Executive*, McGraw-Hill, New York, 1957. (Editor of the Management Development Division of the Research Institute of America, the author asks if you are on top of your job or underneath it. One logical cure for the managerial dilemma of responsibilities that increase without corresponding time available to handle them is greater efficiency. Dividing all managerial activity into three categories—those that are organization-dictated, job-dictated and self-dictated—the author proposes tested techniques for working under pressure, making time for everything, planning and organizing your work for best results. Very practical.)

PART THREE
MANAGING OTHERS

A BIBLICAL PERSPECTIVE
ON MANAGEMENT AND AUTHORITY

The Man in Management—A Biblical View

ANY VIEW of management must be based upon one's view of man. The Bible gives us a clear view of man: "All we like sheep have gone astray; we have turned every one to his own way . . ." (Isaiah 53:6). Thus, as sheep must be directed to move the entire flock along a single path, so groups of people need direction so that their efforts and energies will be directed toward a common goal.

This direction which people need must come from the top. God has ordained this and Scripture teaches it in many ways. Moses set up lines of authority following Jethro's advice which we shall examine more closely (Exodus 18:13-27). The Aaronic priesthood was set up with a high priest and orders of priests under him in varying ranks (I Chronicles 24). The husband is head of the home and a parallel relationship exists in the Church (I Timothy 3:4-5). It is important to recognize that authority flows from the higher levels to the lower in God's plan.

In Christian organizations there appears to be a recurring tendency to forget this. Confusing equality before the Lord with organizational equality, Christian workers may do themselves and their organizations a great disservice by refusing to accept duly constituted authority. We are admonished, "Let every person be subject to the governing authorities" (Romans 13:1). We recall the Roman soldier who asked the Lord to come to his home to heal his servant, saying, "For I also am a man set under authority, having under me soldiers, and I say unto one, Go, and he goeth; and to another, Come, and he cometh; and to my servant, Do this, and he doeth it. When Jesus heard these things, he marvelled at him, and turned him about, and said unto the people that followed him, I say unto you, I have not found so great faith, no, not in Israel" (Luke 7:6-9).

None of this is to imply that all authority, of whatever character, is to be condoned. Authority carries with it great responsibility. Desirable authority is not viewed as being unwillingly imposed, all-powerful, insensitive and unenlightened. Those entrusted with authority are divinely ordained to use it responsibly for His purposes. His ultimate purposes and those of the organization—hopefully one—must be paramount. Sensitivity to the needs of those who are serving as well as those being served is essential.

The nature of authority may be far more complex than is commonly recognized even by those in management. The probability of this seems clear from the comment of Chester I. Barnard, the noted authority on management:

> A person can and will accept a communication as authoritative only when four conditions simultaneously obtain: (a) he can and does understand the communication; (b) at the time of his decision he believes that it is not inconsistent with the purpose of the organization; (c) at the time of his decision, he believes it to be compatible with his personal interest as a whole; and (d) he is able mentally and physically to comply with it.[1]

Not only does Barnard remind us of the complex nature of authority, but also how much it does, in fact, depend upon the attitude with which it is received by those below the person exercising it. Of the forces at work in leadership situations, writers have identified those within the leader, those within the followers, and those within the situation. The life of Winston Churchill, who may not be seriously challenged for the title of Man of the Century, bears graphic evidence of these three types of forces. Recall that after marshalling the morale and the forces of the British Empire in her darkest hour during World War II, he was rejected by his own constituency and replaced as Prime

Minister by Clement Atlee. He returned as Prime Minister at the age of seventy-seven but never forgot the bitter lessons learned at the hands of fickle followers and history. For a definitive review of leadership from a Scriptural perspective, the reader is referred to *A Christian Concept of Leadership* by Richard Wolff.

The Bible has been quoted in numerous instances for its demonstration of management principles. One of the most outstanding examples is the instruction of Moses by Jethro some fifteen hundred years before the birth of Christ (Exodus 18:13-27). Noted below, from the Amplified Version, are these verses along with some of the management ideas and principles they suggest.

13. Next day Moses sat to judge the people, and the people stood around Moses from morning till evening. *(Observation and Personal Inspection)*

14. When Moses' father-in-law saw all that he was doing for the people, he said, What is this that you do for the people? Why do you sit alone, and all the people stand around you from morning till evening? *(Questioning—Discerning Inquiry)*

15. Moses said to his father-in-law, Because the people come to me to inquire of God.

16. When they have a dispute they come to me, and I judge between a man and his neighbor, and I make them know the statutes of God and his laws. *(Conflict Resolution Correction)*

17. Moses' father-in-law said to him, The thing that you are doing is not good. *(Judgment)*

18. You will surely wear out both yourself and this people with you, for the thing is too heavy for you; you are not able to perform it all by yourself. *(Evaluation—of Effect on Leader and People)*

19. Listen now to me, I will counsel you, and God will be with you. You shall represent the people before God, bringing their cases to him, *(Coaching-Counseling Representation Establishing Procedures)*

20. Teaching them the decrees and laws, showing them the way they must walk, and the work they must do. *(Teaching Demonstration Job Specification Delegation; Selection Establish Qualifications. Assign Responsibilities.)*

21. Moreover you shall choose able men from all the people, God-fearing men of truth, who hate unjust gain, and place them over thousands, hundreds, fifties, and tens, to be their rulers. *(Chain of Command)*

22. And let them judge the people at all times; every great matter they shall bring to you, but every small matter they shall judge. So it will be easier for you, and they will bear the burden with you. *(Span of Control Judging-Evaluation-Appraisal. Limits of Decision-Making. Management by Exception)*

23. If you will do this, and God so commands you, you will be able to endure the strain, and all this people also will go to their tents in peace. *(Explanation of Benefits)*

24. So Moses listened to and heeded the voice of his father-in-law, and did all that he had said. *(Listening Implementation)*

25. Moses chose able men out of all Israel, and made them heads over the people, rulers of thousands, of hundreds, of fifties, and of tens. *(Choosing-Selecting Assign Responsibility. Span of Control)*

26. And they judged the people at all times; the hard cases they brought to Moses, but every small matter they decided themselves. *(Judging-Evaluating Management by Exception)*

27. Then Moses let his father-in-
law depart, and he went his way
into his own land.

*So God has appointed some in the church (for His own
use): first apostles (special messengers); second prophets
(inspired preachers and expounders); third teachers, then
wonderworkers, then those with ability to heal the sick,
helpers, ADMINISTRATORS, (speakers in) different (unknown)
tongues.*

— I Corinthians 12:28 (*Amplified Bible*)

CHAPTER 8

WHAT DO YOU MEAN...
"MANAGEMENT"?

THE FAILURE to formulate a sound philosophy of management may have serious consequences for Christian organizations in a number of areas. Interpersonal relations within the organization, for example, are an area coming under increasing attention at management seminars and in professional articles. Behavioral scientists are bringing to bear new discoveries in human relations and their effect upon organizational efficiency. But for years industry has had at its disposal certain fairly well-accepted principles which aided in the handling of interpersonal problems. "Discuss your differences" would seem to be one principle with as much basis in Scriptural teaching as the Sunday school lesson. Yet, observers note, Christian organizations all too frequently fail to recognize such principles.

The matter of handling substandard performance is an even more glaring example. Here secular organizations would seem, generally, to approach the problem in a more "Christianlike" manner than do many of our fine Christian organizations. Performance appraisal and interview procedures go a great way toward meeting this problem. After all, employees have a right to know how they are doing. When they are not doing well, it is critically important that they know this. The Christian organization which, unwittingly, glosses over deficient performance, or pretends it does not exist, is performing an ultimate disservice to the employee as well as to the organization.

A feeling of guilt resulting from confused notions about "judging others" and "seeing only the best in others" at times seems to cripple effective administration at this point. After this there may come rationalization of poor performance as one hears "God is the ultimate judge" or "This is a faith mission, and we can't pay enough to get good help."

Perhaps the responsibility for such a situation lies with the management and a lack of comprehension of management principles, Biblically based, which secular organizations seem to be using far more effectively than our Christian organizations. As one observer commented, "Somehow ungodly men have developed systems of organization which permit them to work together in states of relative harmony and unity, whereas godly men, refusing to admit that these organizational structures are needed, live in states of chaos and disunity. The tragedy of this fact becomes evident when we realize that many of the successful systems of organization under which the ungodly men work and which the godly men refuse to accept are Biblically based."[2]

We have seen enough to accept that *what a manager believes about management is important*. . . . And it is important that he believe something. An executive, in other words, must have a "philosophy of management." Have you?

If you haven't, how about starting with your view of *man;* your view of *work;* your view of *authority;* your view of *organization;*[3] and your view of *management* (its functions and activities; its principles and definitions; its hazards and its opportunities; and its challenge to one who would be a responsible steward of the gifts God has entrusted to his care)?

History records and logic supports the wisdom of knowing *why* you are doing what you are doing. In the approaching era of managerial obsolescence, no one doubts that it will be those leaders who know the reasons behind their actions today who will most likely to be leading successfully tomorrow. "Principles will always defeat practice"[4] is another way of stating the same conclusion. In the midst of a technological and knowledge explosion, with new developments impinging at every point in the managerial process, we need more than ever managers who know *what* management is and *why* it is necessary.

Oliver Sheldon has given us perhaps the most concise statement on the need for a philosophy of management:

> The man at the wheel may be replaced, may be put under a new authority, may be regarded differently by the crew, and may work with different instruments in a different way, but the functions performed remain constant, essential under every conceivable circumstance. It is important, therefore, that we should devise a philosophy of management, a code of principles, scientifically determined and generally accepted, to act as a guide, by reason of its foundation upon ultimate things, for the daily practice of the profession.[5]

As you seek to develop your own philosophy of management, subject it to critical questions. What is the purpose of management—what is its ultimate objective? How do my personal objectives in life fit into this purpose? What are the available means for carrying out this purpose? What are the criteria for selection of the best means and is the means acceptable under these criteria? How will results be appraised? Most important of all—know what you are doing and why.

What Really Is . . . "Management"?

Our reliable friend Webster tells us that management is "the judicious use of means to accomplish an end." One of the most exhaustive studies of the subject of management ever conducted came to a similar conclusion. After reviewing all existing definitions in the literature and analyzing the concepts implicit in the actual behavior of a large number of individuals and groups who have been conspicuously successful in managing their affairs, the American Institute of Management concluded that "management is the art of bringing ends and means together—the art of purposeful action."[6] This definition was held to include every form of human activity covered by any of the terms used to refer to management.

One recognizes that this approach to management is more "purpose-oriented" than many. A definition in common use today proposed by Larry Appley, president of the American Management Association, holds that "management is getting things done through people." This concise definition has the advantage of brevity and of emphasizing the importance of people in any concept of management. Those subscribing to the former definition suggest that deciding *what* to get done and appraising the results are integral parts of the management process. They would then suggest that the former definition ("the art of bringing ends and means together") implies equally appropriate emphasis on the human resources as an integral element of the "means."

Closely allied to the matter of philosophies of management is that of *styles of leadership*, or, perhaps, *methods of management*. A great deal has been written in this area. Contributions range from the "autocrat-bureaucrat-democrat" grouping[7] to the "managerial grid" based on a vertical co-ordinate of concern for people and a horizontal co-ordinate of concern for production.[8] Determined by the extent of concern manifest for each of these two factors, the position of any given management, or the "style of leadership" of a particular manager may be located on the grid. The Theory X - Theory Y philosophy assumes either that employees are indolent, irresponsible and require coercion (Theory X) or that they are creative, imaginative and seek responsibility (Theory Y), with appropriate gradations in between.[9]

One view disagrees with all firm and tightly structured theories, proposing that none of them really fit all situations—rather that combinations will be required depending upon the demands of the position, the character of the personnel and the personality, standards and expectations of the supervisor.[10] This letter view suggests five basic categories from which combinations may be drawn: (1) *laissez-faire:* no structure or supervision given; members set own goals and standards of performance; leader is "first among equals," without authority, a resource man; (2) *democratic-participative:* provides some structure and framework within which members still largely set own goals and standards; leader and advisor with minimum authority; (3) *manipulative-inspirational:* some structure, usually confused and ambiguous; goals set by management with little participation but employees' acceptance sought by "hard sell"; (4) *benevolent-automatic:* activities of group largely structured; relatively close supervision; however, employees encouraged to make suggestions concerning their goals, working conditions, etc.; (5) *autocratic-bureaucratic:* activities of group totally and arbitrarily structured; participation by group in any context totally discouraged; supervision is authoritarian and autocratic; questioning of orders regarded as insubordinate.

Ten Basic Principles

Principles of management have been suggested by writers as long as management has been written about. Any search for primary principles would lead at some point in the endeavor to the American Management Association. Few people have been involved as long or as intensively with the profession of management as its president, Lawrence A. Appley. In his book *The Management Evolution,* "Ten Commandments" are set forth as the most significant principles and truths applying to those engaged in leadership responsibilities. With his permission they are reproduced below:

1. Identify the people of an organization as its greatest asset.
2. Make profit in order to continue rendering service (for profit-oriented organizations).
3. Approach every task in an organized, conscious manner so that the outcome will not be left to chance.
4. Establish definite, long- and short-range objectives to insure greater accomplishment.
5. Secure full attainment of objectives through general understanding and acceptance of them by others.
6. Keep individual members of the team well adjusted by seeing that each one knows what he is supposed to do, how well he is supposed to do it, what his authority is, and what his work relationships with others should be.
7. Concentrate on individual improvement through regular review of performance and potential.
8. Provide opportunity for assistance and guidance in self-development as a fundamental of institutional growth.
9. Maintain adequate and timely incentives and rewards for increase in human effort.
10. Supply work satisfactions for those who perform this work and those who are served by it.[11]

In noting that eight of these ten commandments directly affect human beings, the author concludes that management is unquestionably a matter of individual conduct as a basis for inspiring the finest of thinking and practice on the part of other people.

The Process . . . An Overview

Through substantial expenditure of time and effort, the American Institute of Management developed a fundamental concept of what management is. The ideas embodied in this concept, first presented in its Ninth Edition of a *Manual of Excellent Management*,[12] have drawn very favorable response. More recently they were summarized in their reprint *What Makes Them Excellent?* as follows:

> Management starts with the selection of purposes. It then arranges them in a hierarchy according to their relative importance, selects the means for achieving them, arranges the means in plans which incorporate time schedules, and states objectives and, if possible, quantitative goals toward which progress can be measured. Most goals can be reached by a number of different means, from which the manager must select on the basis of their relative efficiency, morality, or other criteria of desirability.
>
> The general purposes and plans of any undertaking involving more than one person must be communicated to each person responsible for a particular set of contributory activities, and his part de-limited and defined. He, in turn, must communicate the same kind of information to his subordinates, and so on down the chain of responsibility to the last participant. Up the chain must flow information about the progress and outcomes of the various activities. It is essential, to enlist effective participants, that each should have an understanding with his associates and, above all, his leaders as to how his private life purposes will be advanced by his contribution and by improvement in that contribution. There must be supervision to assure timely performance and make necessary adjustments, as well as to insure loyal cooperation and adherence to the general purposes of the undertaking.
>
> No matter what means are employed to achieve a selected purpose, there are inevitably other outcomes, some of which may be irrelevant to, or even inimical to, achievement of the intended purpose. The unwanted side-effects must be minimized.

Their study of excellent managements led the Institute

to identify five previously overlooked areas in which the
men in excellently managed companies surpassed others:

1. More of them have a clear understanding of the
   nature and function of entrepreneurship (creative
   and imaginative review of the assumptions and pro-
   jections on which the endeavor is based) and of the
   need for continuity in it.
2. More of them have a clear, inclusive and fundamental concept of what management is.
3. More of them have a deep and realistic understanding of human nature and motives.
4. More of them have a clear view of the full range of
   their moral responsibilities, and of the need for
   maintaining a balance among them.
5. More of them are intelligently dissatisfied with their
   own results.[13]

What Managers Do

Just what do managers really do when they are managing? In answer to this pertinent question, an anonymous
writer has humorously written:

FUNCTIONS OF AN EXECUTIVE

As nearly everyone knows, an executive has virtually
nothing to do, except—

To decide what is to be done;

To tell somebody to do it;

To listen to reasons why it should not be done, why it
should be done by someone else, or why it should be
done in a different way;

To follow up to see if the thing has been done;

To discover it has not been done;

To inquire why it has not been done;

To listen to excuses from the person who should have
done it;

To follow up again to see if the thing has been done,
only to discover it has been done incorrectly;

To point out how it should have been done;

To conclude that as long as it has been done it might as
well be left where it is;

To wonder if it is time to get rid of a person who cannot do a thing right;

To reflect that he probably has a wife and a large family and certainly any successor would be just as bad and maybe even worse;

To consider how much simpler and better the thing would have been done, if one had done it oneself in the first place;

To reflect sadly that one could have done it right in twenty minutes and now one has to spend two days to find out why it has taken three weeks for somebody else to do it wrong.

As basic as this question is, few definitive answers have been presented. One of the most helpful of these is the work of Louis A. Allen, which reduces management to general functions which encompass all its various activities. As head of Louis A. Allen and Associates, he had researched the field intensively for twelve years, during which he studied nearly four hundred companies and more than twelve thousand managers. In his book *The Management Profession*[14] he analyzes the four major functions of management (planning, organizing, leading and controlling); discusses the nineteen managing activities comprising these major functions; and develops thirty-seven principles of professional management.

As useful as this study has been to top and middle management in industry, it is equally relevant to executives in Christian organizations. While we do not have Christian organizations as large as General Motors, it has long been known that managerial principles are no respecter of size. People, whether few or many, who band together to accomplish a common purpose, in a church or a college, a denomination or an institute or a mission agency, will be more effective in their endeavors if they give careful consideration to the basic principles, activities and functions of management.

Because of its importance to a clear understanding of what managers do, and because such understanding is a requisite for managerial effectiveness in Christian organizations, Allen's outline of functions and activities is presented, with his permission. The discussion following will describe these functions and activities and relate them specifically to problems faced in Christian organizations.

FUNCTIONS AND ACTIVITIES OF MANAGEMENT

PLANNING—Predetermining a course of action.

Forecasting:	Estimating the future.
Establishing Objectives:	Determining the end results to oe accomplished.
Programming:	Establishing sequence and priority ot steps to be followed in reaching objectives.
Scheduling:	Establishing a time sequence for program steps.
Budgeting:	Allocating resources necessary to accomplish objectives.
Establishing Procedures:	Developing and applying standardized methods of performing specified work.
Developing Policies:	Developing and interpreting standing decisions that apply to repetitive questions and problems of significance to the enterprise as a whole.

ORGANIZING—Arranging and relating work so that it can be performed most effectively by people.

Developing Organization Structure:	Identifying and grouping the work to be performed at various positions.
Delegating:	Entrusting responsibility and authority to others and creating accountability for results.
Establishing Relationships:	Creating conditions necessary for mutually co-operative efforts of people.

LEADING—Causing people to take effective action.

Decision-Making:	Arriving at conclusions and judgments.
Communicating:	Creating understanding.
Motivating:	Inspiring, encouraging and impelling people to take required action.

Selecting People:	Choosing people for positions within the organization.
Developing People:	Helping people improve their knowledge, attitudes and skills.

CONTROLLING—Assessing and regulating work in progress and completed.

Establishing Performance Standards:	Establishing the criteria by which methods and results will be evaluated.
Performance Measuring:	Recording and reporting work in progress and completed.
Performance Evaluating:	Appraising work in progress and results secured.
Performance Correcting:	Regulating and improving methods and results.

REFERENCES

[1]—Barnard, Chester I., *The Functions of the Executive,* Harvard University Press, Cambridge, 1964.

[2]—Erickson, Wallace A., *Excellence in Management,* Hillsdale College, November 4, 1965.

[3]—For opposing views of organization as an all-powerful molder of its members versus membership of individuals free to pursue private goals, see *Human Relations in Administration,* Prentice-Hall, Englewood Cliffs, New Jersey, 1961, by Robert Dubin, p. 27; plus views of Chris Argyris, *ibid.,* p. 77. For resolution of views see Charles L. Hughes' *Goal Setting, op. cit.*

[4]—Batten, J. D., *Developing a Tough-Minded Climate for Results,* American Management Association, New York, 1965.

[5]—Sheldon, Oliver, *The Philosophy of Management.*

[6]—"What Is Management?", *Manual of Excellent Managements,* Fifth Edition, American Institute of Management, New York, 1959.

[7]—Jennings, Eugene E., *The Executive . . . Autocrat . . . Bureaucrat . . . Democrat,* Harper and Row, New York, 1962.

[8]—Blake, Robert R., "Breakthrough in Organization Development," *Harvard Business Review,* November-December, 1964.

[9]—McGregor, Douglas, *The Human Side of Enterprise,* McGraw-Hill, New York, 1960.

[10]—McMurry, Robert, *Identifying and Developing Top Executives,* a management seminar outline.

[11]—Appley, Lawrence A., *The Management Evolution,* American Management Association, New York, 1963.

[12]—*Op. cit.*

[13]—*What Makes Them Excellent?*, American Institute of Management, New York, 1965.

[14]—Allen, Louis A., *The Management Profession*, McGraw-Hill, New York, 1964.

CHAPTER 9

WHEN YOU FAIL TO PLAN
YOU ARE PLANNING TO FAIL

Whatever failures I have known, whatever errors I have committed, whatever follies I have witnessed in private and public life have been the consequence of action without thought.

—Bernard Baruch

WE HAVE CHUCKLED, each one of us, on seeing this sign on a friend's desk or on an office wall: "PLAN AHEAD." This choice nugget invariably evokes our sympathy for the poor draftsman who, not unlike ourselves, became so engrossed in his workmanship of the moment that he neglected to anticipate the ending of the card. Failure to "plan ahead," you might say, "loused up" the whole job!

How many of our lives are being "loused up" the same way? How many of our jobs?

Consider for a moment the office manager who saw this sign for the first time on the desk of his assistant. *There's a fellow,* mused the manager, *who can learn a lot from that sign.* Suddenly his mind flashed back to the Saturday on which he himself had hurried off from home to run a few quick errands. Stopping at a friend's office, he dropped off a film he had borrowed for an office meeting. He then crossed the street to the post office. When the three people in line ahead of him were through, he handed over the package to be sent parcel post and asked, in addition, for a roll of five-cent stamps. As he reached for his billfold a thought flashed through his mind. He had intended to stop at the food store in order to cash a check, since he was almost out of money. Sure enough, the two dollars-plus in his pocket wouldn't come close to paying the bill. "Keep the stamps, if you will, please. I find I'm short of cash. I'll drop back later," he offered apologetically.

He pushed his foot down a bit impatiently on the accelerator as he headed for the food store five miles away. *We really don't need food, just the cash—and now I'll have to come all the way back here just to get in line again for stamps,* he thought with some disgust. Ten seconds of time to jot down. "*1.* Cash check at food store; *2.* Drop off film; *3.* Package and stamps at P.O." would have saved him several extra miles, wasted gas, and at least fifteen minutes of time! What a bargain for ten seconds of time! Plan ahead? Oh, yes, the assistant office manager really could profit a lot from this slogan!

The office manager, upon returning to his desk, saw a copy of "A Management Course for Air Force Supervisors" on top of one of the piles of papers on his desk. At the last meeting of his service club the speaker had read an interesting description of the "busy executive" which the office manager had intended to read:

YOU CAN'T WASTE A SECOND

Mr. Carl was a hard-working supervisor. He had enough personnel in his organization to accomplish the workload. In spite of this, his work was rarely done on time. One day Carl excused himself from the chief's staff meeting, stating that he just had to get back to the job. The chief decided to spend the next morning with him.

Next morning when the chief arrived, Carl was talking on the phone, and at the same time signing some forms. He interrupted the phone conversation to greet the chief and, still holding the phone, called to the secretary, "Mary, these forms are signed."

Carl, talking again on the same phone call, thrust the signed forms toward Mary as she entered. His movement pushed a disorderly pile of papers off the corner of his desk. The papers were scattered on the floor by a breeze from an open window and Mary started picking them up. Carl shouted, "I'll think about it and call you back, Oliver." Then he said to Mary, "Don't pick them up; you'll just mix them up worse." He scooped up a paper that was on his desk and handed it to the chief. "There's Don Pitt's idea of how to save about half the time we spend on processing. Wish we had time to try it out. What do you think of it?"

Mary came to Carl's desk. "Bill Evans wants to know if he can start on that priority job right now," said Mary. "Tell him to wait," said Carl. "I haven't time to finish training him, and I just can't trust him to start a job that important without checking it myself."

While Carl was picking up and sorting the papers, Mary brought in some forms. "Mr. Carl, you just signed those on the line for the major's signature, so I typed them over."

"Too much to do," muttered Carl, glancing at the chief. "If you sign them now I'll take them to the major right away," said Mary, reaching.

"I'll take them," said Carl. "The major might want to ask me about them." Carl explained to the chief: "Don and Bob can't do a thing till I run these through. I'll be right back." He dashed out. In a minute he stuck his head in the door. "I forgot to tell you, Mary, don't type that report till I read it. We can get the due date backed up a day. See if the chief wants some coffee. I won't have time for any."

And he dashed away again, but before he went he said to the chief, "No use for Mary to type that report twice. Anybody as busy as I am knows you can't waste a second."

❊   ❊   ❊

The office manager tossed the pamphlet back on the stack, thought momentarily of his assistant whose actions it so well described, failed to connect any of this to his own desk or situation, and returned to his own everlasting task of trying to "catch up."

"Planning," according to Allen, is "predetermining a course of action."[2] The alternative to planning is to act without forethought. Bernard Baruch attributed to this poor practice whatever failures and errors he had witnessed and experienced in private and public life. Some men, who seemed gifted with the ability to act intuitionally, are apparently able to act successfully without conscious forethought . . . without planning ahead. These are rare men. For the great majority, as work expands and becomes more complex, planning becomes imperative if we are to visualize what we want to accomplish and how best to achieve it. Instead of leaving the future to chance, planning is essential in order to *make* happen what we *want* to happen.

Proper planning simplifies the task of the manager. It

makes integrated and co-ordinated effort possible. It increases the effective utilization of available resources, including time. It enhances the opportunity for effective communication within an organization and permits utilization of those closest to the point of action. The importance of planning is underscored by the incorporation of this function into the formal organizational structure of virtually all major industries today.

The barriers to planning are numerous. Emphasis on day-to-day operations almost always pushes planning into the background. *Putting out today's fires takes priority over planning for tomorrow—ironically thus insuring that there will be more fires tomorrow.* The element of uncertainty of the future is a deterrent to planning. Most of us feel more comfortable working within a structured situation with certain and predictable factors. William Oncken, in *Managing a Manager's Time*, describes the unstructured zone of optimum executive action as an "area of ambiguity." Here one concentrates primarily on self-imposed tasks and implements them primarily by delegating responsibility for, and exacting accountability for the results expected.

Making decisions regarding imponderables is not easy or always pleasant. Yet it must be done if we are to exert significant control over the future rather than permit it to control us. The harnessing of analytical, intellectual, imaginative and intuitive capabilities is hard work, particularly in an area which is largely uncharted with familiar systems, techniques and principles. That it must be done for most effective utilization of the available resources is undisputed. "The greatest source of long-term failure for organized endeavors," concludes Allen, "undoubtedly is the failure to plan."[3]

All of us, at one time or another, have given lip-service to planning. We've all seen instances which illustrated that forward planning pays dividends. Yet few of us have actually taken a hard look at the process in order to apply it to our own most critical areas. For Christians concerned with proper stewardship of time, such analysis is imperative.

But many Christians question the Scriptural basis of planning. "Take therefore no thought for the morrow: for the morrow shall take thought for the things of itself" (Matthew 6:34) would seem, they say, to command the opposite. Careful review of this passage reveals that the thought intended is that we not "worry" or be "anxious" about the morrow. Our Lord regarded cheerfulness and joy, and the absence of care and anxiety, as the mark of a true Christian who puts his trust in God.

Further, the admonition in Luke 14:28-30 appears directly applicable:

> For which of you, intending to build a tower, sitteth not down first, and counteth the cost, whether he have sufficient to finish it? Lest haply, after he hath laid the foundation, and is not able to finish it, all that behold it begin to mock him, saying, This man began to build, and was not able to finish.

"But how *does* one plan?" you ask. "Where does one start?" Having never thought carefully about the matter, one is puzzled about where to begin.

Basically, a plan is simply a mental picture of a future accomplishment. No one would consider building a home without a blueprint. This is merely a plan of how the house is supposed to look when completed. Had the draftsman simply pencil-sketched the words "Plan Ahead," this would have forewarned him of the urgent need for recalculation before he made the sign.

For the Christian organization, planning becomes a bit more complicated, yet can be kept amazingly simple with a little effort. Consider the following questions as a simplified guideline for future planning for your organization, department, endeavor or church:

(1) If the present rate and direction of progress continues, where *will* we be in six months, a year, two years, and five—with respect to each major facet of our program? (Forecasting)

(2) Where do we *want* to be at each of these times? (Setting Objectives)

(3) What steps, in what sequence, and what priority of effort, will be required to reach these objectives? (Programming)

(4) What are desirable target dates for accomplishing each of the program steps? (Scheduling)

(5) What resources (manpower; money; equipment) must be allocated to accomplish these objectives? (Budgeting)

(6) Must any standardized methods or techniques be developed and applied to accomplish the objective? (Establishing Procedures)

(7) Must any standing decisions applicable to repetitive questions and problems of significance to the organization as a whole be developed and applied? (Developing Policies)

Forward planning, to be effective, must be done in writing. It is not only practical but highly desirable to have department or division heads initiate the process. This takes advantage of their knowledge of the situation and brings them into the planning process in a way that insures likelihood of maximum participation in the carrying out of the final plan. Since they are the men who will carry great responsibility in execution, it is imperative that they be motivated in every way possible for an enthusiastic response to the plan. The place to begin is with their initiation of the process. They will be much less likely to criticize a plan they played an instrumental role in developing. With the factor of "resistance to change" as dominant as it is in many Christian organizations, this factor of instilling enthusiastic co-operation cannot be overstressed.

One church recently was reported to have set up a "Long-Range Planning Committee" consisting of the chairmen of its four boards (deacon, trustee, education and deaconess).[4] The program called for (1) a review of the church—its Biblical concept, its task, its outreach; (2) a study of the present program and facilities; and (3) a study of the population trends and characteristics of the community. "We're trying to take a good hard look at ourselves," said the chairman. "This is a program of self-appraisal. We hope it will show us where we need to adjust, to change, to alter our methods." Out of its first study have already come significant indications of trends which will require change in emphasis of ministry. Determined not to simply *react* to changing circumstances after they are at hand, this church is *anticipating* change in time to prepare by planning ahead. Its custodian summed up the feeling of many: "We've changed a lot to keep up, but we're going to have to change some more to keep ahead!"

The danger of confusing means with ends must be faced directly, for it places the effectiveness of Christian organizations in jeopardy. The universality of this danger was summarized by Albert Einstein: "Perfection of means, and confusion of goals, characterize our age." For a church, this danger can be seen in the providing of "better buildings and equipment, better materials, better methods, and improved leadership for its work without a clear-cut understanding of what it is trying to accomplish." This, according to W. L. Howse, "leads only to confusion."[5] As one pastor summarized the problem in his church, "We're improving the means. for reaching unimproved objectives."[6] Professor Charles Tidwell, in a discerning article "What Can Objectives Do for My Church?" listed these benefits: (1) tells what is important to your church; (2) gives positive direction to your efforts (you may be static, moving in all directions, or moving backward); (3) sets standards for selecting means; (4) encourages participation in achieving goals, particularly where all participated in establishing them; and (5) measures results, offers a means of measuring progress.[7]

Howse presented so practical a method for establishing objectives and goals for a church that the outline, with his permission and that of *Church Administration* editors, is reproduced as Exhibit A at the end of the chapter. The time required to do an effective job of planning has discouraged many from attempting it. After seeing the benefits to be attained, one is constrained to inquire how any Christian work can afford the time and resources which may otherwise be wasted in unimportant actions. "We're in danger of becoming preoccupied with inconsequentials," said a pastor, as he good-naturedly recounted an episode at the previous meeting of their church board. After spending twenty minutes on final review and approval of a remodeling and addition program in excess of $300,000 the board got down to the matter of responsibility for paper towels, napkins and table coverings. Forty-five minutes later one of the group looked at his watch and observed that the priority of time allotted to these two respective subjects seemed a bit out of line. All agreed and in good humor poked a bit of fun at themselves while returning to more serious matters.

With penetrating insight Professor Tidwell asks, "If your church is making progress now without objectives, how much more progress would it make by having good clear objectives? This is an unknown, a variable. But the proba-

bility is that more progress is made on purpose than is
made accidentally. Objectives are your purpose."[8]

Summing up the case for planning, Edison Montgomery
says, "Successful planning, i.e., clear definition of goals,
determination of methods to move all parts of the organization toward them, a careful review of progress, is the
keynote of success of a voluntary organization. It is necessary to gain and hold the confidence of whatever public
the voluntary organization services."

EXHIBIT A

HOW TO DETERMINE OBJECTIVES AND GOALS
W. L. Howse

How does a church go about determining objectives and
goals? Here are the basic steps to follow:

(1) *Study the nature and purpose of the church.* (Study
selected portions of the New Testament for assistance.)

(2) *State the overarching objective for the church.* (One
group chose as its overarching objective: "to maintain a
vital relationship to God through Jesus Christ and to bring
all men into this same relationship.")

(3) *Study the functions of a church.* (A "function" of a
church has been defined as a basic action which if not
taken seriously alters the nature of a church. A church's
basic functions are *to worship, to proclaim, to educate,*
and *to minister.*)

(4) *State objectives for each function of a church.* Simple
but comprehensive statements of all a church should
accomplish through its functions, such as, for example:

A. *The objectives of worship*

   1. To lead persons to seek God and consciously desire His presence continually.

   2. To lead persons to renew their repentance from
sin and to praise God for His strength and mercy.

   3. To lead persons to engage regularly in prayers of
petition and intercession.

   4. To lead persons to respond in loving obedience to
God's leadership.

B. *The objectives of proclamation*

   1. Etc. . . .

C. Etc. . . .

(5) *State goals related to objectives.* (Goals are means to achieving the objectives, sub-objectives, if you will, whereby progress toward objectives can be measured. They should be reasonable, attainable, set in advance for a fixed period, and written.)

A. The goals to be attained under the objectives of worship.

    1. Evaluate the church's morning worship service and plan specific actions for more meaningful worship experiences for all ages by July of next year.

    2. Enlist _____ per cent of the families of the church in daily worship by December 31, next year.

    3. Provide training in planning for worship (fifteen hours) for all department superintendents, song leaders and pianists of the Sunday school by April 1, next year.

    4. Adopt the statement of objectives and goals.

REFERENCES

[1]–Management Course for Air Force Supervisors, Conferences Outline 10, "How to Plan Work," Part 3, *How to Get the Work Out,* Superintendent of Documents, Washington 25, D. C.

[2]–*Op. cit.*

[3]–*Ibid.*

[4]–*Action,* September, 1965, p. 11.

[5]–Howse, W. L., "How to Determine Church Objectives," *Church Administration,* January, 1964, p. 8.

[6]–*Ibid.*

[7]–Tidwell, Charles A., "What Can Objectives Do for My Church?", *Church Administration,* February, 1966, p. 12.

[8]–*Ibid.*

CHAPTER 10

SO LET'S GET ORGANIZED

*Management's effort to improve its use of human resources
has commanded increasing attention in the past decade.
But no management has as yet solved to its full satisfaction
the sensitive and delicate problem of the effective organization of human effort.*

—Douglas McGregor

MUCH FUN has been poked at the well-intentioned executive whose grand resolves to "get organized" far exceed
the end results. On many a manager's desk the dust has
settled—perhaps significantly—on the cartoon depicting two
managers leaning far back in their chairs with their
feet reclining on the same desk. They seem a bit removed
from their once unquestionably good intentions. "Tomorrow," opines the more industrious of the two, "tomorrow
we've just got to get organized."

The Organization Chart

When we talk about organization structure the picture
that comes to mind is that of an organization chart
on which boxes represent positions in the organizational
structure and reporting relationships are shown by con-
necting lines. Many people fail to realize that the organization chart rarely captures the true picture of an organization and although it may initially have done so, will not do
so for long. The dynamics of organization being what they
are, changes occur within organizations with respect to
communications, decision-making, alignments of opinion
and centers of influence at a rapid rate. These are continuing changes that leave an organization chart obsolete if it
is left untended. Even when up-to-date, these diagrams do
little more than represent who reports to whom, identify

main departments or divisions of work, and indicate relative relationships within the organization.

While these are important, and such information is essential, it is imperative to note that critical areas untouched by these charts will include how the people work together; how information actually flows on the "communications network"; how decisions are made; the extent of the authority residing in each square; what characterizes superior-subordinate relationships; the nature of the tasks to be performed to realize the organizational objectives.

So an organization chart is not a picture of people, but of "paper relationships" of divisions of work to be done, and of lines of responsibility. It is a useful tool for managerial understanding . . . is particularly helpful in orientation of new personnel . . . and must be kept current to reflect the true situation. Webster's definition of "organize" is "to arrange or constitute in interdependent parts, each having a special function or relation with respect to the whole." Louis Allen defines "management organizing" as "the work a manager performs to arrange and relate the work to be done so that it may be performed most effectively by people." Within these definitions the utility of the organization chart, as well as its limitations, becomes clear.

In Christian organizations, as in industry, a surprising lack of delegated responsibility for organization structure is noted.[1] This may account for the lack of organization charts or, where they are found to exist, their obsolescence. Though limited in their scope, this caution is simply a reminder to avoid overreliance, not a suggestion to ignore them entirely. The recognition of such charts as a useful managerial tool is seen in the American Management Association's *Handbook for Position Descriptions*[2] which recommends that a position guide consist of three elements: (1) an organization chart; (2) a position description; and (3) position qualifications.

A new awareness of organizational significance has been forced upon us by automation and such changes within organizational structures as those caused by the introduction of data-processing. The need for attention to this area increases with the size and complexity of organizations. As the number of persons involved increases, the necessity for orderliness in work relationships and assignments also increases. In a properly designed organization, according to Allen, jobs will be "tightly packed with important work and commensurate authority to challenge workers, eliminate duplication, friction and frustration, and provide maximum satisfaction for results accomplished."[3]

"Span of control" is a term designed to express the number of persons over whom a manager is capable of exercising effective supervision. As Christian organizations grow from their inception to maturity, we visualize how this factor becomes increasingly important, frequently without being recognized. The danger in this failure to identify and deal with the problem of maximum effective supervision is that once the optimum number of subordinates is exceeded, the inverse ratio between the number of persons reporting to the manager and the over-all efficiency of the organization may assume serious proportions.

Picture the "entrepreneur-founder," the indispensable one without whose vision, determination and initiative the organization would probably not even exist. Having brought the organization through its difficult years with each key person reporting in a one-to-one relationship to the boss, he finds that the sheer numbers in the organization now make such relationships increasingly difficult, taxing and ineffective. Key men no longer can "get to the boss." When they do, he is snowed "under" by phone calls, nervous about "other worries," increasingly incapable of being available to the men who need him most and in whose hands rests the future of the organization. This is the problem of "span of control."

In industry a common guideline of five to ten has been suggested as the optimum number of subordinates for maximum effectiveness, depending on the situation. Among the factors affecting the situation will be ability to delegate (determining the amount of time left to manage others); complexity of work (affecting frequency of problems requiring consulting); extent of decentralization or separation of those being managed; and the relationships between the subordinates (affecting the extent to which reconciling of differences may be a problem).

The tendency to resist change may be nowhere more evident than in organizational structure. Parkinson's Law (work tends to expand to fill the time available) captures one aspect of this problem. Rather than suggest a change in structure to rectify the problem of his not having enough to do, or request more work, the typical employee will "pace himself" to keep busy. In doing so he is expanding the work to fill the available time. This is a natural tendency in all of us. One consequence of this tendency is to become "activity-oriented" rather than "results-oriented." How many managers would normally consider first what a subordinate had actually accomplished in his time on the job, when discovering that he had not put in the usual eight hours? Many managers who think they are emphasizing results over activity may in fact be doing the opposite by permitting an environment in which the man who organizes his work and leaves on time, or even early, will be viewed with raised eyebrows, suggesting that his loyalty to the organization ought to be questioned. Remember Clarence Randall's advice on what to do with the self-martyred overworked executive—"recognize him for the liability he is." While this, of course, will not be universally applicable, managers in Christian organizations will do well to contemplate its possible implications.

Christian organizations which have men experienced in organizational matters are not common. Of those with prior experience in organization, few will likely have the determination, in the face of pressing responsibilities, to keep up with developments. The accelerating rate of change in management-thinking affecting organizations of all sizes makes attention to this matter urgent. Perhaps no other area poses greater potential for immediate returns in over-all effectiveness ... and over-all effectiveness, in the final analysis, means time.

Delegation

The "entrusting of responsibility and authority to others and the creating of accountability for results"—as Allen defines "delegation"—may be the most important single skill of the executive. In an attempt to dispel some of the confusion which arises over the use of the term, he performs a useful service by defining several key words:

"Responsibility" — the work assigned to a position.

"Authority" — the sum of the powers and rights assigned to a position.

Accountability" — the obligation to perform responsibility and exercise authority in terms of established performance standards.

Allen's definition of "delegation" (entrusting responsibility and authority to others and creating accountability for results) suggests at once where the problems may arise. First there is the strong possibility that responsibility and authority will not be delegated equally. Generally authority is lacking to do all that is implied by the responsibility which has been delegated. This is a serious violation of one of the most important principles of management and should be avoided wherever possible. To ask a man to perform a task for which you are unwilling to give the authority required is to invite unnecessary time wasted in answering questions which will have to be brought back to you. Furthermore, it will discourage the subordinate when he finds that, despite appearances, he had not been entrusted with the authority necessary to do the job he has been given. This contributes to a climate between superior and subordinate which is not conducive to future growth on the part of the subordinate, or to teamwork, or to future successful delegation.

Failure to exact accountability for results takes a toll of executive efficiency and organizational effectiveness that may be far greater than managers imagine. The emphasis on "management by objectives" or "management by results" points to this failure. Who among us, in describing a position, has not outlined the "activities" with which the person in that position is supposed to busy himself instead of describing the "results" he is supposed to accomplish? Check the job descriptions for your key positions, if you doubt this. One of the key determinants in delegation is the fixing of accountability for *expected results*.

Other barriers to effective delegation commonly cited include fear that delegated work will not be done quite as well or in quite the same fashion as it would be if not delegated; fear that it may be done better—creating an unfavorable comparison; lack of understanding of what is required for successful delegation; and lack of organizational definitions of responsibility and authority for various positions (a manager is not likely to delegate responsibility and authority which he is not certain he has!).

Still other barriers to effective delegation were identified by Christian executives in a recent management seminar. They included: inadequate training of subordinates so they could accept delegated duties; fear of insufficient remaining duties; lack of value of own time; and uncertainty as to what ought to be delegated. How a manager determines what to delegate will tell a great deal with respect to the type of leadership he will give his organization ... whether he will be too engulfed in the routine of his job to provide the creative, imaginative, resourceful leadership the times demand. It will tell whether he will expend his efforts and energies putting out yesterday's fires or planning how best to apply today's resources to tomorrow's opportunities.

Many elements in the functions of leadership cannot be delegated. Among them would be the final selection of key associates; final decision-making on major issues; coaching of immediate subordinates; final decisions relating to organizational structure; and the dealing with substandard performance of key assistants. Within each of these, however, there may be matters of routine detail that ought to be delegated wherever possible.

Life is full of paradoxes, and that of the Christian executive is no exception. While most executives are concerned about the pressure of a stacked desk, there is, paradoxically, for some the silent fear of finding themselves with not enough to do.

This is a fear that can strangle delegation, cripple the training of subordinates, dull effectiveness and eventually incapacitate the able executive.

Many managers forget that their own climb up the ladder of success probably would have been jeopardized had they concentrated on making themselves indispensable. Few organizations can afford the price of advancing the man who has made himself irreplaceable by "doing it all himself." There is a spiritual principle here: every Christian leader should constantly be preparing his "Timothy."

The burdens that create tension for our overworked men in executive positions also salve their consciences with a reassuring, if deluding, sense of security. Leo Garel caught one of the extremities of this paradox in his *Wall Street Journal* cartoon. Behind his spacious but immaculate mahogany desk the imperious executive sat strumming his fingers. "You know how valuable my time is, Miss Grey," he said to his secretary standing in the doorway. "Couldn't you please find me something to do?"

We need not fear that managers whose foresight in planning and determined delegation brings them dividends of extra time will have difficulty in deciding how to spend those bonus minutes. The most important of their "unstarted projects" will be waiting, ready to go.

Establishing Relationships

How does one "create the conditions necessary for mutually co-operative efforts of people?" Discussions of this point in industry tend to polarize around such ever-present problems as "line-staff relationships." In general the "line" people make decisions and issue orders, while the "staff" people provide services of a special nature found necessary to the effective functioning of line personnel. While this problem may not be faced in most small to medium-sized Christian organizations, it may be found in many medium-sized to large organizations. While the magnitude and complexity of this problem are beyond the purview of this book, it is a great mistake to overlook its significance. An excellent reference work consisting of a compilation of twenty-five selected readings under the title *Human Relations in Administration* is recommended.[4]

It would be easy to assume naively that Christian organizations have no problems in human relations. "How could they?" asks the uninformed outsider. "Aren't they in the Lord's work, after all?" Unfortunately, many discerning observers of Christian organizations are concluding that they are particularly afflicted with critical deficiencies in this very area. It may be that every reader will know of one—a friend or acquaintance—who has gone to work for a Christian organization only to be surprised, amazed, or permanently disillusioned by the treatment of people in the organization. As one who has served on several of their boards puts it, "The paths of Christian organizations are strewn with the corpses of their friends."

While the authors do not pretend to have the answers, there is no question that it is time to face the problem. We talked earlier about certain of the principles of personnel management which secular organizations attempt to follow. We asked why Christian organizations refuse to follow them, when they are seen to be not only Biblically based, but also capable of solving problems. Let us trust that this situation has resulted simply from lack of knowledge and also remember that low aim, not failure, is a sin.

If organizational relationships are simply the "rules established to ensure effective teamwork among people working together," it should be evident to every Christian executive that ultimate success and resultant blessing in the performance of his task may be affected to a critical degree by his comprehension of and effective inplementation of such rules.

REFERENCES

[1]—In Louis Allen's study of two thousand management positions (*op. cit.*) less than ten per cent indicated any delegation of responsibility for organization itself.

[2]—*Op. cit.*

[3]—*Op. cit.*

[4]—Dubin, Robert, *Human Relations in Administration*, Englewood Cliffs, New Jersey, 1961.

CHAPTER 11

IF YOU'RE A LEADER...LEAD

If the trumpet give an uncertain sound, who shall prepare himself to the battle?

—I Corinthians 14:8

How much is written, and yet how little seems to be understood, about the subject of leadership. It takes little imagination to conceive that the best organized endeavor, equipped with the finest materials, following the latest methods, and backed with adequate financial support, would be critically hampered without the leadership required to combine all of these elements into an effective endeavor.

If leadership is that important, how much do we know about it? Curiously, the answer appears to be—not much. The reason, according to Jack Taylor in *How to Select and Develop Leaders,*[1] is that leadership involves people and we don't know much about people. One of the top authorities in the field of leadership and management development for the past two decades, Taylor lists many pages of selected definitions of leadership by recognized experts. Few bear more than passing resemblance to the others.

While we have discussed various leadership *styles* (from autocratic to participative), we have said nothing about what might be called its *qualities* (such as drive, initiative and persistence). Some have written about what leaders should *be* (decisive, fair, etc.), while others have surveyed *what "followers" sought* in their leaders (thoughtfulness, honesty, proficiency, etc.). Some experts have studied what

123

leaders should *know* (human relations, management principles, organization objectives, etc.) and what they should *do* (think creatively, plan, organize, follow-up, etc.).

The list of definitions is never-ending, it seems, and each appears to be as valid as the next. For our purposes the "leading" with which we are concerned is that function of management defined by Louis Allen as "the work a manager performs to cause people to take effective action."[2] He breaks this function into five component activities—decision-making, communicating, motivating, selecting and developing.

Decision-Making

As with other management skills, that of decision-making has undergone much scrutiny in recent years. Many books and articles have been written on the subject. Consulting firms specializing in the areas of problem-analysis and decision-making have developed within a matter of a few short years. More and more seminars and definitive treatments of the subject of management deal with this area at some point. It is called by some the most critical of all management skills.

In their systematic approach to decision-making, Kepner and Tregoe enunciate seven basic concepts involving a number of procedures:[3]

1. Setting objectives against which to choose.
2. Classifying objectives as to importance.
3. Developing alternatives from which to choose.
4. Evaluating alternatives against objectives to make a choice.
5. Choosing the best alternative as a tentative decision.
6. Assessing adverse consequences from the choice.
7. Controlling effects of the final deicision.

Many who have taken the one-week seminar offered by Kepner-Tregoe and Associates have commented particularly on the new insights gained from the first two concepts. Asking themselves "What do I want to accomplish and in what relative priority?" has caused many to face these crucial questions for the first time. While not promising to give easy answers, the authors do claim for this system the significant benefit of providing a system for marshalling a large body of data concerning multiple alternatives in a fashion that permits comparison against a range of objectives of varying importance.

Managers who have studied this and other decision-making processes are finding that they provide not only an extremely valuable tool to assist in their own managerial choices but also a framework within which to question subordinates regarding their basic procedures in arriving at their decisions. The asking of the right questions concerning objectives, for example, at the right time can be a most effective form of leadership.

Not the least of the advantages of having a system is the time saved by eliminating needless forays into irrelevant areas. The sharpening of objectives at the outset provides a profitable guide to relevant as opposed to irrelevant pursuits.

While the list of helpful hints for making decisions could be long, and involved, there are several which have warranted comment by many writers on the subject:

1. *Don't make decisions under stress.* It's better to delay a decision than to make it when you're angry, upset or under great pressure.

2. *Don't make snap decisions.* The spur-of-the-moment decisions are merely guesses unless they are backed up by adequate data.

3. *Don't drag your feet.* The decision must be made sometime. Putting it off usually results in adding it to an already overflowing inventory of unfinished business.

4. *Consult other people,* particularly those who will be affected by your decision.

5. *Don't try to anticipate everything.* You'll never have *all* the facts, so you'll have to base your actions on those facts available at the time a decision is required.

6. *Don't be afraid of making a wrong decision.* No one is omniscient. There is risk involved in every decision.

7. *Once the decision is made, go on to something else.* You gain nothing by worrying about past decisions and you lose the capacity to give your full and dispassionate attention to other important decisions.[4]

There are many stumbling blocks in the pathway of effective decision-making. One of the most serious is the apprehension of the risk involved—the fear of making a mistake. "Readiness to risk failure," said George Spaulding, "is probably the one quality that best characterizes the effective executive." All of us recognize the fact that we learn fastest through the mistakes we have made. Yet we somehow fail to see the connection between this and the courage required to make a difficult decision. If experience is the best teacher, and we learn by doing, we as managers should welcome the opportunity of making decisions. Particularly should this be so with a loving and understanding Heavenly Father to look to for guidance each step of the way.

We look again at the old proverb: "Not failure, but low aim, is sin." Our attitude toward failure may need re-examination. It is difficult to find a great leader whose life was not marked with significant failure. It was what they did with their failures that counted!

"Who should decide?" you ask. This question is another way of asking at what level decisions ought to be made. It is an important question because you may not have heard of "delegating up." This occurs when your assistant brings a problem, which he should be deciding himself, to you for an answer. When you unwittingly take over for him and work out his problem, he has succeeded in "delegating up." If you were asked the proper level at which that decision ought to have been made, your answer would not only be embarrassing to you, it would be revealing as to your understanding of several areas of leadership.

The maxim that decisions should be made at the lowest level consistent with good judgment is based on the principle of holding decisions as close as possible to the facts and data upon which they are based. The principle of efficient operation also enters in when considering the uneconomical aspects in use of talent and funds when leaders spend their time making decisions which their assistants are capable of making. In the utility of time, this manager will thus be denying himself time to do other more important things. Caution must be exercised, of course, to insure objectivity. Where emotional factors may exist, those intimately involved in the details of a situation will very possibly lack the objectivity required for sound judgment.

Certain decisions, although capable of being handled effectively by assistants, may have an important bearing on the over-all effectiveness of the organization. Close control over such decisions will be imperative for the executive.

That decision-making is really a process with identifiable steps has come as a surprise to many managers. Those who manage "by intuition"—and who hasn't at one time or another?—may be inclined to scoff at the idea of analyzing the process of arriving at decisions. "I look at the facts and decide what needs to be done!" is the answer—a common over-simplification—which such people give when queried as to how they make decisions.

The distinction between decision-making and problem-analysis is commonly overlooked. The two are often confused as when a person facing a choice between alternative courses of action (decision-making) says, "I have a problem. Should I let the office staff go home early today and work Saturday morning, or should I keep them on this afternoon and not call them in Saturday?" This manager faces a decision between alternatives, not a problem in the problem-analysis sense. The most obvious distinction between the two procedures is that problem-analysis produces an explanation that can be verified because the event (or cause) has already taken place. Decision-making produces answers that cannot be verified because the actions will take place in the future, which is always uncertain.

Most writers do not distinguish between these two procedures. Content to let the term "decision-making" cover both, they *do* agree on the importance of *identifying the real problem*. A problem well-stated is half solved. This frequently means first identifying the apparent problem ... then checking the facts carefully (who? what? when? where? why?). Once the real problem is ascertained, possible solutions are generated from which the choice of the best one is made, and a course of action laid out to implement it.

"Examine the decisions a manager makes," says Louis Allen, "and you see accurately reflected there his ability to reason, his powers of observation, his attitude toward people. His decisions spell him for what he is—positive, logical and forward-looking, or uncertain, confused and defensive. Great undertakings find life in sound and venturesome decisions; failure decides its own illogical and inconsistent grave."[5]

Communication

"There's a lot of communication these days on the subject of communication," commented a participant wearily as he left the conference.

"Sure is," replied his companion, "but this fellow just doesn't understand our situation."

The foregoing conversation occurred following a three-day seminar on "Communcation." It highlights one of the most interesting aspects of a vital management skill. Allen summarizes it with his opening remark on the subject: "A great deal of information is conveyed about communication without much real understanding taking place as to what is meant."[8] By defining management-communicating as "the work a manager performs to create understanding," Allen bridges the gap where many conferences have foundered.

Immediately following the three-day seminar noted above, an informal critique was held with the conference co-ordinator and three of the participants. When asked what they felt would have improved the conference the most, all three agreed that the answer was probably "better communcation." The speaker, a well-known expert in the field, heading a department of communications for a major university, had failed to communicate with his own audience on a subject of his acknowledged expertise. He knew the subject thoroughly; his theoretical presentation was flawless; but the net effect on his hearers was "He just doesn't understand our situation." The speaker had failed to present his subject in a way that was meaningful to his audience. He had projected facts or knowledge, but not understanding. For his message to have meaning for those who heard, it had to be relevant to their problems. They had to see it in the light of their own situation.

How often is the physical act mistaken for the final communication? "I delivered the message!" came the angry response to the manager's query as to why his request had not been carried out. True, the message had been delivered. Had there been communication? The tone of the voice in the response provides a clue to the probable answer.

The notice posted on the lunchroom door announcing the shortening of the coffee-break periods, with a listing of dubious reasons for the action, could easily be mistaken for communication. The "funny faces" scribbled over it the next morning may bear mute testimony to its failure to establish real understanding.

The letter written in haste, in anger, or solely from the writer's point of view may be thought of as communication. In reality, it may be wasted effort. *Wasted effort.* Ah, here's the rub . . . and perhaps a key to the management of time. Anything that is wasted effort represents wasted time. The best management of our time thus becomes linked inseparably with the best utilization of our efforts. Thus the management of time becomes a matter of *how* we do *what* we do *all* the time.

Our value systems and emotions have been described as major road blocks in the pathway of effective communication. They form a sieve through which all attempted communcation must pass. The stronger our feelings the more formidable this road block becomes. Selective listening is a term which has been applied to this factor which filters all we hear and tunes out everything except what we want to hear.

Everyone has tried, or heard about, the experiment in communications distortion by a group standing in a circle. A specific message is started from one point and passed from person to person around the group. The comparison of the final version with the original usually provides a source of real entertainment as well as a great lesson. This lesson has not been lost on those charged with responsibility for communications in large corporations who constantly review the levels through which important communications must pass and the possibilities of distortion.

The importance of the meaning of words, when viewed from the perspective of varying value systems, must be considered. Not the least of our problems lies with the different meanings given by different persons to the same words and phrases. An appreciation of this factor will enable a manager to take significant steps toward insuring more effective communications.

Of all the factors in communication which are being viewed and reviewed by social scientists, management consultants and chief executives, perhaps none merits critical attention more than the art of *listening*. Through the valuable contributions of men such as Dr. Ralph Nichols of the University of Minnesota and Dr. Wiksell of Louisiana State University, we are seeing for the first time what poor listeners we are; what the main reasons seem to be; and what we can do about it. Who would have thought, before Dr. Nichols enunciated it so clearly, that one of the greatest causes of poor listenership is the failure to capitalize on the difference between the time it takes to *say* words and the time it takes to *think* them! Our minds race at two to three times the speed of the spoken word. Thus we are continually "tuning in and out" on the conversation, and frequently staying off the beam so long that we lose the subject and miss some of the key points. The following remedy is suggested: use this time constructively. Evaluate what the speaker is saying; his qualifications for saying it; the extent to which his statements are supported by the facts. Anticipate his next point. When the speaker misses a point occurring to you, ask a question to confirm its relevance. What might have been an apathetic response thus becomes one of vital interest, and probable benefit to the speaker.

Emotional reactions to loaded terms, failure to resist distraction and psychological deaf spots—these may prevent good listening.

A fatal problem is that of ruling out a subject at the outset as uninteresting or devoid of value. A good listener has been described as a winnower—listening closely because he is always looking for something that will increase his knowledge and understanding or that he can use in a conversation or a speech. "And his reward," said Roger Farley at the American Management Association's Management Course, "is that he almost invariably finds it."

Bruce Larson, whose *Dare to Live Now*[7] was described by Catherine Marshall as an honest, provocative, fresh approach to Christianity, asks a most discerning question: Do you communicate without trying? Or do you try without communicating? Noting that people respond more to *how we feel* about them than to *what we say* to them, the author points unerringly to the "great mistake we make in thinking that our knowledge or insight is the greatest gift we can give to others." Often we bring them much further, he concludes, when we listen eagerly to what they are trying to say about themselves and their problems. We affirm their worth and dignity by taking them seriously.

Recently a large industrial concern, convinced that improved employee communication should bring about improved employee relations, decided to look at itself in the mirror.[8] To each member of management went a questionnaire, designed to be a self-audit for the thoughtful review of executives. Participants were assured that the quiz was planned neither to affront nor embarrass. It was described simply as a "sincere attempt to invite management to evaluate its own performance and see what basic changes or improvements might be made." These are the questions (the reader should make his own application, mindful that profit, unions and size are important factors in the industrial world):

1. Are top management members sincerely interested in the employees, their needs and their problems, or is top management interested exclusively in the profit picture?

2. Do members of top management make a sincere attempt to keep in touch regularly with the rank-and-file viewpoint? Or does it accept (from selected representatives) their interpretation of how employees feel?

3. Do the firm's employees *know* the members of top management? By name, or possibly just by sight? (This one is obviously phrased more for the big company than the small, but it could come close to home there, too.)

4. Have we (as members of management) made an effort to tell employees about our management problems, and have we ever asked for employee co-operation in solving them? Or do we handicap ourselves by the belief that employees have nothing constructive to contribute?

5. Have we made any *real* provision for giving our employees useful information regularly—such as bulletin boards, newsletters, face-to-face meetings, supervisory sessions, etc.? Or are we too busy being management officials to care?

6. If we *do* communicate—in short, if we answer the preceding questions with a *Yes*—do we check the effectiveness and credibility of what we do and say? Or do we simply take the employees' acceptance of the employer's veracity for granted?

7. Have we, as members of management, introduced a practical, workable method by which employees

can get their views to *us?* Or do we assume that we know instinctively what's on our people's minds?

8. Do our company's employees feel they belong? If the answer is *Yes*, just what are we doing specifically to make them feel a part of the company? If pressed, could we actually prove it?

9. Does our top management encourage employee participation in sports programs, the credit union, employee brainstorming groups, as well as political and civic activities, just to pick a few at random? Or do we pass over all this with the idea that it has no meaning?

10. Finally, a triple-headed query: Does our company have a satisfactory grievance or complaint facility? Do our people know the appropriate steps to take if the supervisor's decision—or our own—is considered unfair? Does our management actually review the "gripes" that employees make?

The executive author of the questionnaire assured his respondents that this was by no means a complete self-audit for management. He said, however, that the questions "may at least lay a groundwork for reappraisal," and added, "Remember this: An adroit union organizer would have determined all of the points of our vulnerability in *every single one* of these areas. Frankly, have we?"

Motivation

How does one get people to do what has to be done? This question, which has been asked since people first worked together to unify their efforts, has yet to be answered definitively. Social scientists in the management field have focused much attention on it recently. Sensitivity-training is designed to make one more aware of the feelings of others. This is surely basic to understanding how to motivate, how to inspire, how to infuse a spirit of willingness to perform effectively.

For years the most effective motivation in industry was assumed to be the use of arbitrary authority and the threat of its use to withhold benefits or to impose penalties. Time and motion studies became the vogue for maximizing working efficiency. Then came the realization that machinery and processes would run no better than people *wanted* them to. Slowdowns, strikes, apathy and disinterest could not be controlled with time and motion studies. The famous studies at the Hawthorne Works of Western Electric Company showed that simply putting a worker in a test situation provided sufficient interest and stimulation to ensure increased productivity even in the face of increasingly disadvantageous working conditions. Understanding what gives his people a feeling of recognition and importance is of primary importance to the manager. People who sense in their leader the ability to help them satisfy their needs will follow him willingly and enthusiastically.

Lack of unanimity in preferred leadership styles reflects, to some degree, difference of opinion over concepts of human relations. The manager who is task-oriented primarily will not consider human relations to be as important a factor in performance as the people-oriented manager. Motivation is affected by such factors as degree of identity between organizational and personal goals, security, sense of fulfillment and accomplishment, relations with associates and superior, and income requirements.

Participation in the decision-making process has been identified as a strong factor in motivation of performance. A person who has had a part in developing a policy will be less likely to be critical of it ... more likely to support it and to work for its successful implementation. The value of communication in developing motivation has often been overlooked. "Motivation to accomplish results," says Louis Allen, "tends to increase as people are informed about matters affecting these results."

The importance of these understandings was emphasized by Robert Dubin in his description of organizations as "assemblages of interesting human beings . . . and the largest assemblages having anything resembling a central coordinative system called management."[9] Comprehension of the human problems of administration begins with such understanding.

Among the most important principles of human behavior of interest to managers are:

1. Behavior depends on *both* the person and his environment.
2. Each individual behaves in ways which *make sense to him.*

3. An individual's *perception of a situation* influences his behavior in that situation.
4. An individual's *view of himself influences what he does*.
5. An individual's behavior is influenced by his *needs*, which vary from person to person and from time to time.[10]

In articulating these extremely useful principles, Paul Buchanan cautions the manager who wants to understand and work effectively with others to give attention to the individual *and* to the situation he is in *and* to the relation between him and the situation. The behavior of a person thus might be changed in any one of three ways: by changing the person through development of skills and knowledge; by assisting him in changing the situation in which he works through modification of procedures or assignments; or by a combination of these.

The need to "make sense" out of one's situation and behavior accounts for the origin and spread of rumors when information is not available to employees. They will tend to make up or guess at the facts and to make assumptions as to why the information is withheld. Conclusions that "management is just not interested in us" or "things must not be going well" are drawn much more often than managers realize. Perhaps no single fact of the managerial world makes the need for adequate communication more imperative than this principle. The worker who has access to information about a situation doesn't have to take time to speculate about what the situation "must be." He can devote his energy to accomplishing the task before him, with less likelihood of acting on false assumptions and being plagued with uncertainty and indecision.

Previous experience is known to be a primary factor in our perception of a situation. Since the individual combination of one's experiences is unique, the result of highly individualistic points of view is inevitable. For the leader this underscores the importance of listening and observing to enhance the likelihood of being able to change behavior. Objective analysis and sympathetic understanding of differing points of view may be the manager's most effective tool in bringing about improved performance of employees.

Psychologists say that to be completely objective about what we do is impossible. We cannot, they say, remove our inner concerns and self-concept from our actions. We can be more objective by attempting to understand how our actions reflect our own concerns and by taking this into account in our relationships with others. And perhaps more importantly, we should realize that others also will behave in ways that protect and enhance their inner feelings.

The line from the Gospel melody, "Only to be what He wants me to be ..." reflects an innate need of man to strive to become what he is capable of becoming (through Christ). Social scientists and philosophers have called this a striving for self-realization. Moving down the scale of the commonly referred-to "Maslow hierarchy of needs," we find ego needs (sense of self-worth); social needs (belonging), security needs (protection from harm, loss of employment); and finally physiological needs (food, activity, air, sleep). These needs are generally depicted in a hierarchy, with physiological needs at the bottom and self-realization at the top, to indicate that a need at one level tends to operate as a primary source of motivation when needs at a lower level are sufficiently satisfied for that person.

In Christian organizations there appears to be a tendency to assume that motivation must never be examined since this would border on a violation of the admonition not to judge. Not only is this admonition wholly applicable to management of Christian organizations, but the failure to make any effort to understand or to utilize basic human motivation principles may be depriving our organizations of a principle source of energy, enthusiasm, creativity and resourcefulness. This is not to gainsay the great importance of dedication to the Lord's work. Nothing can replace this imperative ingredient. But, assuming that this quality is present, what about the rest? Must we assume they are *not* important? Or should managers recognize that we are mortals all and that the pursuit of our calling ought to be what Paul Tournier calls "an adventure in living"? When recognition of the established needs of man enables a manager to make one's work more meaningful and more fulfilling, it would seem that to deny him these satisfactions could hardly be a part of God's design.

At this point the question of "manipulation" appears. "How does the manager separate motivating from manipulating?" is a question that has arisen in Christian management seminars. When, for instance, might a request to a mailing-room clerk to stay overtime for several hours, couched in terms intended to persuade him to want to perform this unattractive task, be viewed as manipulative rather than motivational? While it seems that this is one of the questions to which there are no simple answers, some guidelines may be suggested. Where the ultimate objectives of the organization are clearly spelled out, where department goals have been articulated and reconciled directly with the over-all objectives, and where the employee's ultimate commitment and his personal goals are in accord with these objectives, such problems should be answerable.

In the "how to" area of motivating employees, we sometimes learn from cautions of what not to do. One of the best summaries of how to "demotivate" employees comes from an industrial psychologist and personnel consultant:[11]

1. Never belittle a subordinate. (Destroys sense of self-worth and initiative.)
2. Never criticize a subordinate in front of others. (This temptation appears under pressure. Destroys rapport.)
3. Never fail to give subordinates your undivided attention. (Personal, undivided attention from time to time is imperative. Self-respect disappears with the realization that the boss will never give his undivided attention.)
4. Never seem preoccupied with your own interests. (Gives impression of selfishness and of manipulation of others for your own purposes.)
5. Never play favorites. (Quickly destroys morale of group.)
6. Never fail to help your subordinates grow. (The feeling that the boss is one who fights for his men is a great motivator. Inform them of openings, opportunities, and never hold them back out of self-interest.)
7. Never be insensitive to small things. (What may seem insignificant to you may be extremely important from the employees' perspective.)
8. Never embarrass weak employees. (While toleration

of weakness in a key position often destroys the initiative of strong people, the manager must take care never to deal with this problem through causing embarrassment.)

9. Never vacillate in making a decision. (Indecision at the top breeds lack of confidence and hesitancy throughout an organization. Add this to other problems above and motivation may be irreparably damaged.)

Virtually all consultants in the personnel field relate a manager's success as a leader and a motivator to his sincerity in demonstrating his concern for his subordinates. "The best way to motivate a subordinate," according to Dr. Feinberg, "is to show him that you are conscious of his needs, his ambitions, his fears and himself as an individual. The insensitive manager, who is perhaps unintentionally aloof, cold, impersonal and uninterested in his staff, usually finds it very difficult to get his people to put out an extra effort."[12] His seventeen ways for a manager to show his concern and sensitivity for (hence to motivate) employees follow:

1. Communicate standards, and be consistent. (Minimizes misdirected effort and motivates through known goals.)

2. Be aware of your own biases and prejudices. (Emotional reactions often color what should be objective judgment.)

3. Let people know where they stand. (Do this consistently through performance review or other methods. To withhold this critical information does the ultimate disservice to your organization—through demotivating the employee—and to the employee, who needs and has a right to know.)

4. Give praise when it is appropriate. (Properly handled, this is one of the most powerful motivators—especially in difficult performance areas or areas of anxiety.)

5. Keep your employees informed of changes that may affect them. (This doesn't mean telling them all company secrets, but you evidence your concern for them by informing them of matters in which they are likely to have a direct interest.)

6. Care about your employees. (Not only *be* attuned to the individual needs of those under you, but *communicate* this awareness.)

7. Perceive people as ends, not means. (To avoid the charge of using people for your own selfish goals, remember Thomas Cook, the explorer. He named a newly discovered island after the first man who spotted it. He regarded each man on the crew as a partner in the adventure and they loved him for the feeling of usefulness he gave them as individuals.)

8. Go out of your way to help subordinates. (A little extra effort, some personal inconvenience, goes a long way with subordinates in confirming the feeling that what they are doing is important to you . . . and that they are, too. Be sure the help you are giving is what is needed. Remember that in correcting an error, improving a deficiency, or strengthening a weakness, you must first know the individual. This may take hours of hard thought and experience.)

9. Take responsibility for your employees. (A part of caring is the willingness to assume some responsibility for what happens to your employees. Be involved in their personal failures as well as their successes. A part of you fails or succeeds with them. As Frank Stanton, CBS president, asks his key people, "Is this the best job you and I can do together?" He thus demonstrates that he assumes partial responsibility and that he really cares.)

10. Build independence. (A supervisor who cares seeks to loosen and gradually drop the reins of supervision. Encourage independent thinking, initiative, resourcefulness.)

11. Exhibit personal diligence. (The most highly motivated leaders have the most highly motivated followers. Example is one of the best motivating factors.)

12. Be tactful with your employees. (Consideration, courtesy, sense of balance, appreciation and sensitivity to the views of others—all are important in dealing with employees.)

13. Be willing to learn from others. (Give new ideas a friendly reception, even when you know they will

not work. This will encourage more creative thinking, and future ideas that may work.)

14. Demonstrate confidence. (Review any doubts you
may have about your department, your staff, your
projects or your company alone and in private.
Demonstration of the leader's confidence builds
confidence in his followers. Show by your behavior
and speech that you are confident the work can be
done; confident of your own responsibility; confident of their ability to handle the job.)

15. Allow freedom of expression. (Assuming your subordinates are reasonably competent, relax your
vigil and allow them freedom to do things their way
occasionally. Be more concerned with ultimate results than with methods of accomplishing them.
This makes assignments much more interesting and
challenging for subordinates.)

16. Delegate, delegate, delegate. (Assuming your people are competent and ambitious, delegate to them
as much of your burden as you can. Recognize that
pressure motivates and that most of us are not
challenged to perform close to our capacity. Then,
as much as possible, let them ride with their own
decisions, learn from their own mistakes, and revel
in their own successes.)

17. Encourage ingenuity. (The lowest-paid clerk may
be ingenious. Challenge creativity by urging subordinates to beat your system of doing things. If
your filing system isn't satisfactory, don't change it
yourself; have your clerks and office manager tackle
the job. The challenge to improve on the boss's system may bring surprising results.)

Perhaps one of the least recognized but most important
principles in motivation is that of "participation in decision-making." In viewing the hierarchy of needs one can
readily appreciate that once an employee or a group of
employees have adequate income to satisfy their physiological and security needs, participation in the decisions
affecting their work may provide an effective means of
satisfying all three of the ascending needs in the hierarchy
—social needs, ego needs and self-realization.

One of the significant steps in researching this area
occurred in 1954 when the Foundation for Research on

Human Behavior invited a number of business concerns, research agencies and other organizations to participate in a series of seminars on the subject of "Leadership Patterns and Organizational Effectiveness."[13] The basic principle of participation, as stated by Louis Allen, holds that "motivation to accomplish results tends to increase as people are given opportunity to participate in the decisions affecting those results."[14] This participation requires systematic provision for consultation with subordinates in those matters directly related to their jobs. The psychological result of asking subordinates for suggestions, recommendations and advice is the development of a "mutuality of interest" with a powerful motivational impact.

Selecting People

The importance of skill in selection of people has doubtless been overlooked in Christian organizations as it has in industry. More attention has often been paid to the purchase of a new machine for the shop than to the selection of a new executive representing an investment over his career of perhaps ten to one hundred times as much.

Still no one denies that of all the assets available for furthering the organization's objectives, none is more precious than its people. Without them the rest would be for naught. As a steel magnate commented, "you may take my industries, my properties, my money—but leave me my men and I'll gain them all back and more."

The high cost of making mistakes in selection of personnel is reflected in the number one management goal of the General Motors Corporation:

> The careful selection and placement of employees to make sure that they are physically, mentally and temperamentally fitted to the jobs they are expected to do; to make sure that new employees can reasonably be expected to develop into desirable employees, and so that there will be a minimum number of square pegs in round holes.[15]

Milton Mandell, in his authoritative work entitled *The Selection Process: Choosing the Right Man for the Job,* cited this particular management goal as notable for a number of reasons: its reiteration of top management's belief in the importance of the selection process; its emphasis on placement along with selection; its inclusion of physical, mental and temperamental attributes as job qualifications; its recognition of the concomitant role of supervision and training in developing "desirable employees"; and its understanding that selection is never perfect—there will always be "a minimum number of square pegs in round holes." An employee may fail for an infinite variety of reasons, and no selection program can evaluate or anticipate all of them.[16]

With employers hiring 750,000 new employees every month in the United States, or 9,000,000 a year, it is not surprising that the high cost of mistakes in selection has been evaluated with increasing concern. Estimates of the cost of replacing a clerical worker range widely, from fifty to two thousand dollars for the simplest job to two hundred and fifty to seven thousand dollars for positions requiring higher skills.[17] For a comparison of costs in the middle managerial levels, the replies of 136 survey respondents indicated an average cost of $6,684 for hiring one salesman, and 33 of the 136 assessed the total tangible cost to the company, should the salesman prove unsatisfactory after fair trial, at more than ten thousand dollars.[18]

Generally overlooked by Christian organizations is the distinction between selection and placement as well as the comparable difficulty of the latter process. Whereas in selection the applicant must be measured both against general job requirements and against other applicants, in placement he has to be measured against the different requirements of several positions. Questions arising with respect to placement criteria include the relative importance of skills, promotion opportunities, interests, kind of supervisor, and type of colleagues the applicant will find most congenial. One helpful analysis suggests that the ambitious employee will be influenced most strongly by career opportunities, whereas workers with low levels of aspiration will tend to value placement based on interests and on quality of supervision. Colleagues will be least important to the lone wolf and most important to the gregarious type of employee. Placement in accordance with interests and needs is more important to men than to married women or young girls because the job generally is more central to the men's happiness.[19]

While the failure to determine the qualifications desired in a given position is common, no less an error is the setting of standards too high for the job. Such a mistake can lead to an unnecessary reduction in the number of applicants, increased recruiting costs, delays in filling a key position, and ultimately excessive turnover when those selected find the work beneath their capabilities.

Virtually all writers in the field agree on the vital importance of selecting applicants with the greatest potential for growth in the organization's particular environment and their placement where that potential will be developed to its fullest. As Mandell concludes, "Clearly, no organization can itself survive and grow if it fails to hire employees with the capacity for self-development and to provide an atmosphere conducive to achievement."[20]

While detailed analysis of the factors entering into sound selection and placement procedures is beyond the purview of this book—for this Mandell's comprehensive work is highly recommended—the factor of identification of potential requires comment. A common error is to assume that effective performance at one level within an organization necessarily is predictive of probable success at a higher level. While much support may be marshalled for the conclusion that the most dependable criterion for predicting success is past performance—"You ask me to predict what a man will do . . . tell me what he has done" —the dangers of overemphasis in this approach are being questioned with increasing regularity.

Dr. McMurry, of the McMurry Company, observes that while rank-and-file employees are a good source of middle-management material, this group is a poor place to look for top-management candidates. He cautions that only rarely is it possible to move a person up more than two or three levels successfully because the qualities that tend to make successful top managers, such as breadth of perspective, genuine self-confidence and self-reliance, as well as compulsive drive, are not those which will be welcomed at middle-management levels.[21] Dr. Smith of Harvard summarized the conclusions of a nationwide survey on this subject:

> Men seemed to lose their effectiveness on moving from one level to another, or on moving from jobs that were predominantly staff to jobs that were predominantly line, and vice versa. For example, it is sometimes difficult to move from local functional officer to headquarters functional officer; from division general manager to headquarters staff officer;

from headquarters staff officer to division manager; from headquarters staff officer to chief executive.

Changes such as these involve a difficult emotional adjustment because they involve new status relationships with others. Some men apparently find it easier to master a new function than to acquire a new status. For example, a treasurer of a fairly large chemical company became its sales manager with great success. On the other hand, a successful regional production manager in a metal products company had great difficulty when he was made headquarters manager of production.[22]

Two psychiatrists commenting on these same differences concluded:

Success in administration on higher levels has one significant difference from that on lower ones—namely, that there is no superior to please, or to manipulate when one reaches the policy-making top. Therefore, for the top man, the motivations and skills must be at least in some ways different from those of the men who work under him. He must, for one thing, have a considerably greater degree of maturity and independence of judgment. There is a large, and open, question as to whether these traits will be found at the top in the event that they are lacking on the way up the ladder. Further . . . there is considerable doubt whether the personality characteristics contributing to success in climbing up the ladder are always conducive to good leadership once a man has arrived at the top.[23]

In his treatment of executive selection, Mandell cautions that "there are no unqualifiedly great executives, as a look at the executive qualification checklist following will convince us. The most capable is the one who is at the right place at the right time and who is judged by those who admire his strengths and are not affected by, nor ignorant of, his weaknesses. As many of the 'mistakes' made in executive selection result from errors in the attributes being sought as from errors in evaluation."

EXECUTIVE QUALIFICATION CHECKLIST

A. Effectiveness with people.
    1. Represents his organization effectively.
    2. Gains the confidence of his superiors.

3. Handles human relations problems so that morale and productivity are improved.
4. Assigns employees to jobs in which they can perform best.
5. Is willing to accept subordinates who are not "yes men."
6. Gets the full co-operation of other units.
7. Deals effectively even with people who are opposed to him.
8. Gets people who work for him to want to do their best.

B. Decision-making ability.

1. Anticipates how people will react to his decisions and proposals.
2. Absorbs new data and concepts quickly.
3. Recognizes the need to get the facts before making a decision.
4. Makes decisions on the organization of his unit which promote co-ordination and efficiency.
5. Is willing to change his program and methods in order to keep up with current needs and development.
6. Makes decisions on technical problems which keep in mind the latest developments.
7. Takes a broad approach to problems.
8. Spots the key parts of complex problems and does not get lost in minor details.
9. Thinks of new approaches to problems.
10. Is willing to accept necessary risks.

C. General executive ability.

1. Delegates appropriately.
2. Knows how to check on results.
3. Sets priorities effectively.
4. Uses his manpower effectively.
5. Corrects situations when they need improvement and does not wait for an emergency.
6. Plans carefully.
7. Handles the administrative details of day-by-day operations competently.
8. Is successful in presenting budget requests for his unit.
9. Selects highly capable subordinates.

10. Relates his work to the work of the whole organization.
11. Takes into account the public relations implications of his actions.
12. Handles many different problems effectively at the same time.
13. Works efficiently under frustrating conditions.
14. Balances interests in details and in board problems.

D. Personal characteristics.

1. Considers divergent and new points of view.
2. Is flexible in his approach to problems.
3. Is reliable in what he says.
4. Is willing to accept responsibility.
5. Adjusts easily to new situations, problems and methods.
6. Keeps his head in an emergency.
7. Works to fix things that go wrong instead of making excuses.
8. Gives an honest report on a problem even if it hurts him personally.

E. Stamina and good health.

F. Organizational and technical knowledge required for decisions, control and representation.

G. Obviously, for those of us in the Lord's work, a primary qualification is the man's personal, consistent relationship with Jesus Christ.

Many suggested steps in the selection process are available. Most well-managed organizations subscribe to certain basic steps:

1. *The Job.* Make sure the job is necessary. If it cannot be reassigned, then streamline it *before* looking for a person to fill the position. Summarize the functions, responsibilities and organizational relationships in a position description. Certain characteristics will be essential for the person filling this position. Summarize them in a position qualifications list. Included will be such personal specifications as age, sex, family and related matters; educational requirements; and previous experience.

2. *The Search.* Determine whether candidates will be

sought outside as well as inside the organization. For considerations such as morale and past experience, promotion from within is generally recommended. Lack of qualified material or an advanced stage of internal conflict may dictate extending the search outside the organization.

Christian organizations frequently face difficulty in locating candidates for key positions. Unlike their counterparts in industry, they are restricted by strong restraints which discourage their hiring from other similar organizations. Generally the compensation is not comparable to similar positions in industry so that the motivation for one coming in from the business world must be direct service in the Lord's work and the satisfactions resulting therefrom. Few Christian organizations seem able to tap their total potential resources with respect to the search for managerial talent. Board members, staff, key donors and friends are all potential and logical sources for suggestions. Better means should be sought for making known the various organizational needs.

3. *Review Applications.* Applications should be screened in a systematic manner to determine those which meet the qualifications and requirements for the position. At this point the benefit of clear and concise statements of job requirements and qualifications becomes apparent. The better the job done with these, the easier the task of winnowing out applicants not qualified. Screening at this point saves expenditure of time and effort in testing and interviewing unsuitable candidates.

4. *Administer Tests.* Various tests properly used by trained specialists have been established as an invaluable tool for the selection process. Professional skills are required for interpretation of test results and in successful programs test results are used as indicators and aids in the selection process, not as the final determinant. Among the many industries using extensive test programs are General Motors and Sears, Roebuck and Company. The latter finds that tests are useful in identifying characteristics in a manager *before he is hired* which could otherwise be learned only through years of observation. Sears looks for the following characteristics in its managers:

Mental Ability: Of prime importance here is the speed with which a person can learn; a good manager learns quickly.

Administrative Skill: A manager should be able to make objective decisions without becoming emotionally involved. He should be co-operative, tolerant and open-minded about other people. He should be able to show firmness in dealing with others.

Sociability: A manager should *want* to work with other people and to help them. He should meet people easily and take the initiative in group activities.

Stability and Predictability: Key characteristic of a manager is a cheerful and optimistic outlook. He should feel confident of himself.

Ambition: To be an effective manager, a person should want to better himself.

Conduct Preliminary Interviews: After obviously inadmissible candidates have been screened out, serious interviewing of the narrowed field is possible. The initial interviewing may be done by the manager himself or by his personnel department or an assistant. Questions designed to obtain the most helpful information at this point include:

1. *Why are you interested in this job?* Is there a real interest in the position? Does he know enough about the position to match his own capabilities against what the job requires? Or is he merely looking for a job? If he doesn't have a good answer to this question, help him make up his mind before you continue with him.

2. *Which, of all the jobs you have held, did you like best? Why?* Here the interviewer can get a good indication of the person's real interests. It is important that the candidate really want the job—that he be really interested in it.

3. *Where do you expect to be at the end of your first year with us? Your fifth?* This should give the interviewer an idea of what the applicant thinks of himself and his own abilities as well as indicate his energy, drive and ambition.

4. *What are your strongest characteristics? Your weakest?* The applicant's own estimate may be surprisingly informative. The interviewer can follow up any leads with further questioning.

5. *Would you go back to the last job if offered the opportunity? Why or why not?* Answers to this question

should be appraised carefully. They should bring out information that will tell a great deal about the person being interviewed.

6. *Investigate Previous History.* Before finalizing his selection, the manager should look into the previous history of the applicant. How did previous employers regard him? Why did he leave? Was he ambitious and hard-working? Did he have trouble with his boss? Answers to these questions, generally most easily asked over the phone, will be most helpful. When these replies are compared with two or three similar responses from other former employers, a pattern can usually be put together which will form a forecast of anticipated behavior.

7. *Conduct Final Interview.* This should be a detailed interview conducted by the manager himself to provide final assurance that this is his man and also to provide the candidate a final opportunity to size up the manager as the person for whom he wants to work. Frequently multiple interviews are arranged to provide maximum possible exposure to each other and to the job requirements.

8. *Provide Physical Examination.* Health is important to the manager facing the responsibilities and pressures in today's managerial positions. Not infrequently such exams reveal conditions which were unknown to the applicant and they may also provide information which is essential to the employer either for his final decision of selection or maximum utilization of talent and capability following the selection.

9. *Maintain Follow-up on the Job.* While this point will be developed more extensively a bit later, it is stressed here for emphasis and because it ought to be thought of as the final part of the selection process. Too often new hands are treated as old; orientation periods are treated as testing periods; training is overlooked in the search for results. Alert the team to the new member before he arrives so that they can make him feel accepted, too. See that he is properly introduced and assign someone to be available at all times to answer questions of any nature, if you cannot do so yourself. This will smooth the adjustment period considerably and solve minor problems before they can become serious. Train the man by continuous counseling and careful appraisal of his performance. "The first few weeks are critical," cautions Allen. "If we can help the

SUMMARY OF JOHNS-MANVILLE SELECTION PROCEDURE

To Warrant Employment

an applicant must meet the standards at each step of the selection procedure, and must qualify for the job in all five respects.

The qualifications to look for at each step are shaded:

See if he appears to have qualifications.

Look for evidence he has the qualifications.

STEPS IN SELECTION

Screening Interview

Reject if:
Lacks essential qualifications.

Application Form

Reject if:
Lacks essential qualifications.

Employment Tests

Reject if:
Test scores are too low, or too high.

Reference Check

Reject if:
Record in prior job disqualifies — poor job progress, or couldn't get along with people.

Comprehensive Interview

Reject if:
Too little ability, personally unacceptable, poor work habits, no real interest, or immature or unstable.

ANALYSIS & DECISION

Reject if:
Picture as a whole is not favorable.

Qualifies in all respects.
Employ on favorable medical report.

JOB QUALIFICATIONS				
Capability for job	Acceptability to others	Perseverance - Industry	Interest in *this* job	Maturity - Stability

149

new man adjust successfully to his new job and team mates, we will have then accomplished a major responsibility as a professional manager."

While specific organizational requirements make it impossible to prescribe any fixed pattern or procedure for universal application, the Johns-Manville selection procedure has been cited by Mandell for a number of reasons including:

Use of basic selection methods: interviews, application form, tests, reference checks, medical examination.

Delineation of major areas of job qualifications and their relation to each selection method.

Differentiation between rejection (if applicant possesses less than desired minimum of a characteristic) and selection (if he has the minimum or better).

Use of each selection method as a rejection factor to reduce expense and to insure that each applicant finally considered qualifies in terms of the characteristics measured by each method.

Arrangement of the steps in the selection procedure according to expense, with the least expensive methods used first.

Collection of reference and test information before the comprehensive interview.[24]

We spoke earlier of the high cost of mistakes in careless selection and placement procedures. The loss of managerial time is, of course, part and parcel of the same waste. When Jack Taylor observed that "the deepest pitfall any organization can dig for itself is to put small men in big jobs," one of the things he must have had in mind was the colossal waste of executive time inevitably involved.

Developing People

Personnel development has been described as "helping people improve their knowledge, attitudes and skills."[25] Managers somehow overlook the vital role this function plays in effective leadership. Even if key positions were filled with people who brought to them all the knowledge, attitudes and skills required, the normal growth of the organization and the consequent job enlargement would make it imperative that serious attention be given these attributes. The rate of development of concepts and techniques in the field of personnel alone adds a still more critical dimension to the picture.

Strange, then, that so little attention is being paid to an area so important to the future of our Christian organizations. Many executives in religious organizations realize in a vague way that there are needs, but haven't taken time to identify them specifically. Others frankly state that their organizations have "no training programs worthy of the name."

A strange paradox confronts us at once. Jack Taylor identifies it by observing that the manager's degree of confidence in his selections of keymen will inevitably affect his approach to development. The more casual the selection procedure, the greater the confidence in the selection, and the more ready for leadership responsibility he considers his selectees to be. Conversely, the more careful the selection process, the less confidence he has in the selection, and the less ready for leadership responsibilities he believes his selectees to be.[26] This paradoxical attitude would seem to mark the poor start for the certainty of a worse ending.

To aid in the search for a requisite, relevant, realistic, feasible leadership-development program, Taylor suggests a simple basic formula:

That which leadership requires, minus
The requirements which the selectees already need, leaves
The selectees' total development needs.

Out of this remainder, then . . .

That which the selectees can develop, minus
That which they cannot develop, leaves
The selectees' practical development needs.

Out of these needs, then . . .

That which is common to all selectees comprises
The group's development-program content;
That which is common to one selectee comprises
The individual's development-program content.

The subjects revealed by application of this formula will constitute the leadership-development program. Broken down into classifications pertaining to knowledge, skills, or attitudes, they represent *what* you will be endeavoring to develop and will determine *how* you will proceed. Definitions of these three essentials of leadership development are:

Knowledge: cognizance of facts, truths and other information.

Attitudes: reactions to things, people, situations and information.

Skills: the ability to put knowledge into practice.[27]

Hundreds of millions of dollars are spent in industry each year on management development, seminars, evening courses, job-rotation, and in-company training programs. The end results of this massive investment have come under increasing scrutiny. In terms of improved knowledge, attitudes and skills of managers, questions are being raised as to the net worth of the programs. The concern for answers in this area is increased by dire predictions that within the next ten years there will be a critical shortage of management talent.

Reasons being advanced for this phenomenon include blind reliance on formalized programs not attuned to real needs of the managers or to the ultimate objectives of the organizations. Another failure is seen in the tendency to produce functional specialists rather than generalists with a broad overview of management. Years of experience in confining or highly structured jobs may diminish the supervisor's capability of responding to the unstructured and unpredictable demands of the managerial position.

Training *away* from the job can provide essential perspective, new insight and additional knowledge. It cannot, however, provide a substitute for direct application of managerial knowledge and skills to the responsibilities *on the job*.

Finally, there is undue emphasis on promotion, rather than development, as the chief end of such programs. The motivation which should be sought in this situation is the desire to excel in the managerial performance in which we are engaged.

A fatal defect in many development programs is the lack of full support from top management. Without realizing that their own actions have doomed the ultimate success of the program, many executives have encouraged their keymen to participate while showing in one way or another that they would never do so themselves. "Too busy," comes the quick answer. But when top management is "too busy to bother," it doesn't take middle management long to get the idea that it probably isn't important enough for them to bother, either. The discerning executive who recognizes the full impact of personal example as well as the importance of keeping current with new developments in the field of management, does not hesitate to take the first step in this vitally important area.

If, as Louis Allen cautions, the human material with which the manager works is at once the weakest and the strongest of the resources available to him, it is small wonder that the most successful executives place personnel development among their highest priorities.

REFERENCES

[1]—Taylor, Jack W., *How to Select and Develop Leaders*, McGraw-Hill, New York, 1962.

[2]—*Op. cit.*

[3]—Kepner, Charles and Tregoe, Benjamin, *The Rational Manager*, McGraw-Hill, New York, 1965.

[4]—Shapp, Harold, "Trained Men," Vol. 44, No. 3, *Executive's Digest*, March, 1965.

[5]—*Op. cit.*

[6]—*Op. cit.*

[7]—Larson, Bruce, *Dare to Live Now*, Zondervan Publishing House, Grand Rapids, Michigan, 1965.

[8]—Newcomb, Robert, and Sammons, Marg, "Communications Clinic," *Personnel*, March-April, 1966.

[9]—Dubin, Robert, *Human Relations in Administration*, Prentice-Hall, Inc., Englewood Cliffs, New Jersey, 1961.

[10]—Buchanan, Paul C., "The Leader Looks at Individual Motivation," *Looking into Leadership Executive Library*, Leadership Resources, Inc., Washington, D.C.

[11]—Feinberg, M. M., *Effective Psychology for Managers*, Prentice-Hall, Inc., Englewood Cliffs, New Jersey, 1966.

[12]—*Ibid.*

[13]—"Leadership Patterns and Organizational Effectiveness," Foundation for Research on Human Behavior, Ann Arbor, Michigan, 1954.

[14]—*Op. cit.*

[15]—Hendrix, A. A., "Interviewing Techniques," *Industrial Medicine and Surgery*, Vol. 19, 1950.

[16]—Mandell, Milton M., *The Selection Process: Choosing the Right Man for the Job*, American Management Association, New York, 1964.

[17]—Gaudet, Frederick J., *Labor Turnover: Calculation and Cost*, Research Study 39, American Management Association, 1960.

[18]—Mandell, M. M., *A Company Guide to the Selection of Sales-*

men, Research Report 24, American Management Association, New York, 1955.

[19]—Kuhlen, Raymond G. "Needs, Perceived Need Satisfaction Opportunities, and Satisfaction with Occupation," *Journal of Applied Psychology*, Vol. 47, 1963.

[20]—*Op. cit.*

[21]—McMurry, Robert N., *Identifying and Developing Potential Top Executives*, the McMurry Company, Chicago.

[22]—Smith, George A., *Managing Geographically Decentralized Companies*, Graduate School of Business Administration, Division of Research, Harvard University, Boston, Massachusetts, 1958.

[23]—Cohen, Mabel Blake, and Cohen, Robert A., "Personality As a Factor in Administrative Decisions," *Psychiatry*, Vol. 14, 1951.

[24]—*Op. cit.*

[25]—Allen, Louis A., *The Management Profession*, McGraw-Hill, New York, 1964.

[26]—Taylor, Jack W., *How to Select and Develop Leaders*, McGraw-Hill, New York, 1962.

[27]—Allen, Louis A., *The Management Profession*, McGraw-Hill, New York, 1964.

CHAPTER 12

WHO'S IN CONTROL?

It is always a great mistake to command when you are not sure you will be obeyed.

—Mirabeau

Management Controlling

Louis Allen defines "management-controlling" as "the work a manager performs to assess and regulate work in progress and completed." Activities and terms involved in the subject of control include:

Establishing Performance Standards: establishing the criteria by which methods and results will be evaluated.

Performance-Measuring: recording and reporting work in progress and completed.

Performance-Evaluating: appraising work in progress and results secured.

Performance-Correcting: regulating and improving methods and results.

Assess: to weigh and appraise.

Regulate: to adjust; to return to a predetermined course.

Performance: the act of doing work.

Results: the outcome of performance.

Methods: the way work is done.

To the manager who is unaccustomed to thinking in managerial terms, the subject of *control* may seem the least familiar and the least comfortable of all those with which he must deal. In Christian organizations it may, in fact, be purposefully avoided because of a supposed conflict with God's leading.

Twenty-five executives of Christian organizations met in Chicago at a Christian management seminar at which this question was raised: "What about the aspect of manipulation when we seek to motivate and persuade our people to follow a certain course of action?" A companion question was also asked: "How does God's leading fit in?"

Although we must admit the danger of oversimplification, the sound approach to the critical area of control within Christian organizations would appear to be that applied in industry. David W. Ewing, associate editor of *Harvard Business Review*, found that "an administrator's attitude toward the manipulation of subordinates has momentous consequences for his career." It has a bearing on whether the work of assistants will bear their stamp or his; it determines the number of people the manager can utilize effectively; if affects the general atmosphere and morale of the organization (since "frustration, guilt, resentment of authority, and self-confidence are all partial outgrowths of the control relations between manager and managed"); and, finally, the extent and quality of manipulation will have a bearing on the total effectiveness of the organization.

Ewing summarizes the spectrum of control possibilities by citing several elements he chooses to designate as follows: force, hidden persuasion, open persuasion, and the final alternative of job definition. Conceding that the first three techniques may be found necessary in given situations, Ewing concludes that the man with a managerial mind experiences a gnawing discomfort from using any technique of manipulation. He yearns for something better.

This question brings us to a fourth approach: defining the job and its purpose, picking men carefully and giving them all possible support, then trusting to their own ambition and judgment to see the work through. The boss says, in effect, "Here is a *job* that needs to be done." It may be tough, demanding, or even unpleasant, but that makes no difference. The boss believes that once the other man understands the nature of his mission, he will supply his own motivation and, if technically qualified, do best as "his own boss." It is vital, however, to ensure that the subordinate is never excused from the responsibility for producing according to exacting requirements. In fact, his independence from detailed supervision may even lead to higher expectations.

Thus one answer to the problem of manipulation is found in the managerial technique of "management by job assignment." The assumptions underlying this technique are of importance to its thorough understanding:

1. The people who staff organizations are of unequal ability.
2. The manager believes he can pick good men for the job.
3. The administrator assumes he is as dependent on other people as they are on him.
4. He believes himself justified in letting the power of creative relationships work in ways that he may not understand.
5. He feels no compunction in placing heavy burdens of judgment and decision-making authority on subordinates' shoulders.
6. The supervisor assumes that it is good for employees to be genuinely concerned about the operations of the enterprise despite the probability that he himself will have to accept interruptions of his office schedule, "talking back," and conflicts of opinion between managers and workers.
7. The manager assumes that most people like to be challenged to use their ingenuity and that, in taking this approach, he does not risk his effectiveness or popularity.
8. The manager assumes that he can be loyal to the organization and to the people in it without having to agree with people's decisions about the way they do their jobs.
9. The manager or supervisor assumes that he cannot really put himself in another employee's place.

An issue which is omnipresent but seldom faced in Christian organizations is that of tolerance of waste and inefficiency. At this point consultants caution against overemphasis on efficiency. It can result, they argue with persuasion, in even greater and more devastating types of waste—that of personal abilities, initiative and morale.

Why control? Management is "getting things done through people." Therefore it seems evident that planning, organizing and leading may not be enough. The adage about "the best-laid plans of mice and men . . ." is relevant at this point. Follow-through is essential if the end results of all your efforts as manager are not to be left to chance. From the Scriptural view of the man in management and all known philosophies of leadership, the fallibility of man stands out as an accepted verity. Controlling, or "assessing and regulating work in progress or completed," therefore becomes an essential. Seeking to apply the principle of responsible stewardship, Christian organizations place even greater importance on this last of the four functions of management.

Control may be exercised in several different ways. Most common, of course, is that of *personal inspection*. Many situations demand this type of control because of their peculiar nature, whether it be urgency, variability or lack of criteria for evaluation. The great disadvantage of personal inspection is that it limits the scope of the manager to that which he can personally observe and appraise. Furthermore, it may tend to discourage subordinates by making them feel that they are being "watched" or are "not quite trusted for the final results." In organizations which are undergoing rapid growth, it is not uncommon for the founder to bring his enterprise through its initial period of growth with effective supervision of a personal nature. When the organization grows too large for him to supervise personally, its effectiveness may be jeopardized if he fails to adjust his methods.

Management by exception simply means control through reports of what is going wrong. Since the methods to be used and the results to be expected have been predetermined, no reporting is required while progress continues according to plan. When problems of sufficient import arise, the manager is alerted. Thus much time is saved for other and more important considerations which ought to be occupying the manager's time.

The Allen Principles of Control offer a most interesting perspective on two aspects of this important subject.

Principle of Least Chance: "In any given group of occurrences, a small number of causes will tend to give rise to the largest proportion of results." In any group a few will produce the most work; a few will produce the most errors. In a fund-raising compaign it is not uncommon for twenty per cent of the donors to contribute eighty per cent of the funds. The typical list of donors will reveal not too dissimilar results. The value of this principle lies in the capability it gives us to maximize results by concentrating our efforts on the minimum resources which hold the greatest potential for end results. Industrial management is urged by modern consultants to be "opportunity-oriented," that is, to concentrate its efforts and resources on its principal opportunities. Thus major expenditures of resources are committed where maximum results can be expected. This approach is particularly recommended to offset the tendency to become "problem-oriented" or to spend our efforts and energies in putting out yesterday's fires, rather than in furthering our progress toward our objective. William Oncken, in his film *Managing a Manager's Time,* produced for the American Management Association, divides expenditure of time into three categories: (1) refining yesterday's answers to last year's problems; (2) finding answers today that were due yesterday; (3) taking action today that was planned yesterday for results expected tomorrow. The action that counts, of course, is in the third category.

Principle of Point of Control: "The greatest potential for control tends to exist at the point where action takes place." Consider for a moment the relative efficiency of management control at the top where the chief executive receives reports, evaluates, decides upon corrective action, and issues instructions which must pass through several layers of organization to the point of action. Compare this with control established at the supervisory level immediately above that at which the action occurs. In terms of optimum expenditure of time and effort there is no question that the control point ought to be established as close to the action as possible. Considerations of personal qualifications for exercise of such control including capacity for sound decisions, are of course important.

Caution should be advised against emphasis on results to the exclusion of methods. Results are in the past *and* therefore beyond correction. While corrective action is possible to prevent recurrence, more effective action will include control over methods which make possible timely corrective action. Another caution warns against the *quantity* of information generated for control purposes without regard to its *quality*. The emergence of data-processing threatens to make more complex an already difficult problem—that of more information than managers can digest and utilize. As Louis Allen succinctly put it: "Sound control depends upon the development of the minimum amount of information that will do the job, and reporting it quickly enough to be useful."

A word about accounting and financial information is in order because this is the area with which most managers in Christian organizations have least familiarity. Courses in "Finances for Nonfinancial Executives" and "Accounting for Nonaccounting Executives" are now common, emphasizing the need for comprehension of principles in this area by those who manage. Control of finances is thought by many Christian executives to be the most critical area of their responsibility.

In order for top management to place its maximum emphasis *on the future* where it belongs, according to the consensus of informed opinion, careful analysis of how, where and when to apply control techniques is mandatory. Many books have been written on the subject of management-reporting. Good judgment will answer most of the questions if proper attention is given to the subject. Suffice it to say that no successful manager can afford to overlook it.

Establishing Performance Standards

To assess or appraise the results of an organized effort requires some knowledge of how actions ought to be performed. To know when actions are performed incorrectly requires that one know how they are performed correctly. Simple though this principle appears to be, it is seldom heeded. Rare is the manager who has consciously thought his way through this critically important area.

One of the great values of performance standards is the objective basis they provide for appraisal. Other benefits to be obtained from their use include the encouraging of initiative; the encouraging of self-appraisal and self-development; and the providing of a basis for effective reporting.

Among the commonly mentioned rules for effective performance standards presented by the American Management Association are these:

Joint developments by supervisor and employee (to insure understanding and reduce areas of disagreement).

Statement of basic results expected (including defining of all important duties, responsibilities and functions of job and specifying of results desired in all areas).

Identification of accurate means of measurement.

Clear statement to avoid misunderstanding.

Measurement of both quantity and quality of work performed.

Attainability.

Provision for periodic revision.

The difficulty with aspects of performance thought not to be quantifiable is generally overrated. Persistence in efforts to quantify such factors often yields results. An example of nonquantitative standards occurs in Civil Service Form CSC 125 as follows (task statement on left; standard on right; at bottom the general aspects of position not measurable in quantitative terms):

1. Represents the bureau at a variety of meetings attended by representatives of departments and agencies.

1. Opinions expressed, judgment displayed, general conduct and demeanor, and accuracy of information released are at sufficiently high levels to reflect credit upon the bureau and the commission.

GENERAL PERFORMANCE
Requirements

A. Is reliable. Can be depended upon to carry out assignments promptly and in accordance with instructions, procedures, etc., and to be ready and available for special assignments.

B. Applies time, interest and energy to duties without wasting own time or time of others.

C. Is co-operative. Willingly assists and works with others in the total interest of the organization. Observes office rules and regulations and works through channels.

Checklists for Performance Standards (developed by the United States Civil Service Commission):

1. Have you broken down the work assignment into its separate tasks?

2. Have you prepared task statements which describe the "doing" parts of the job in "action" language?

3. Does each task statement contain only one significant duty?

4. Are the especially important tasks underlined?

5. Do performance standards state *not* outstanding, *not* perfect, but *satisfactory* performance?

6. Does each performance standard tell *how much, how well, in what time, or in what manner?*

7. Does each performance standard state the *full range* of satisfactory performance, so that everything above standard is outstanding and everything below it is unsatisfactory?

8. Is each task fully covered by enough standards to provide a complete and well-rounded check on how well the task is being performed?

9. Is the language simple, definite and easy to understand? Has every effort been made to avoid "weasel" words in favor of objective, concrete words and phrases?

10. Has the employee participated in developing his task statements and standards of performance? Do the supervisor and the employee have the same idea of what *each* of the standards mean?

The following checklist suggests type of measures that may be appropriate to various tasks and may help you to make your standards more specific:

I. HOW MANY — Specific number of units of work.

II. HOW SOON — What is the time within which the task should be started or completed?

III. WHAT RESULTS, QUALITY — What happens when an adequate number of work units has been produced?

IV. WHAT METHOD — How must the work be done?

V. WHAT KNOWLEDGE — What must the employee know to perform the task?

VI. APPEARANCE OF ADEQUATE WORK — How does an adequate unit of work look?

VII. HOW MANY ERRORS — Number of percentage of work units in which the errors are permitted.

VIII. WHAT RESULTS, ACCURACY — What happens when accuracy of the work is adequate?

IX. PERSONAL CHARACTERISTICS — What attitude, appearance, voice characteristics, etc., are necessary for adequate performance?

Perhaps the most telling tribute to the importance of performance standards was paid by Larry Appley of the American Management Association in the A.M.A. management course:

> A great experience awaits the executive or supervisor who calls together his immediate subordinates for a conference to develop standards of performance. In answer to the question "What are the major activities of the job that should be measured?" he will be amazed at the difference in opinions and at the length of time it takes to get agreement.
>
> The first objective of the group is to list on the blackboard the major segments of the job. The development of the list may take an hour; it may take half a day. Regardless of the length of time, it is a most important development. Having developed a list of the major segments of performance, the discussion leader should now ask the group to select one of those segments for which to develop standards. . . .
>
> Standards of performance should deal with the basic results that management desires and which are actually secured through individual performance . . . Any manager should have statistics available to tell him the progress he is making toward the accomplishment of basic results.
>
> People who are responsible for making reports and records are constantly begging units of the organization to tell them what is wanted. . . . This very careful detailed study tells them what the executive needs to know.
>
> One of the greatest benefits of this work on standards of performance is not the finished material that goes on the blackboard, but the discussion that takes place in getting it there. . . . It is a process of discovery.
>
> Patient, continuous, well-organized effort is required to produce the type of standards that will create the attitudes and produce the performance desired.
>
> Experience shows that standards of performance can be written for any job.

Louis Allen considers the psychological factor in preparation of performance standards to be fully as important as the mechanical considerations. The first purpose, he points out, is to make people want to excel. A standard not only tells the worker how well he is doing; it makes him want to improve. As a result of the identification of outstanding performance, a strong motivation for excellence is built into the system. Similarly, the identification of inadequate performance provides a strong incentive to excel. Group needs should not be overlooked in the recognition of individual accomplishment lest this encourage concentration on individual effort to the detriment of the over-all objective.

We need not feel that Christian organizations are alone in overlooking the use of performance standards; it is well known that industry, with the exception of the more forward-looking organizations, has long been lacking in this area. Other areas of American life yield even more discouraging observations. "The Pursuit of Excellence," the Rockefeller Brothers Fund report published in the *America at Mid-Century Series*, declares:

> If we ask what our society inspires in the way of high performance we are led to the conclusion that we may have, to a startling degree, lost the gift for demanding high performance of ourselves.

John Gardner, former president of the Carnegie Foundation, produced a most discerning work on the general subject of whether excellence is possible in a democracy. Entitled *Excellence*, the book carries on its front cover this trenchant observation:

> This book is the first on a hotly controversial subject, one that deeply concerns a growing number of people: the lack of high standards of performance in too many areas of American life, the reasons for it and what can be done to encourage excellence.

That we as Christians must face this challenge should be self-evident. Responsible stewardship of the resources in personnel, facilities, equipment, capabilities and opportunities which God has entrusted to our organizations demands that we impose the highest standards on ourselves to insure maximum utilization of these resources for His purposes.

While we give lip service to this principle, as a practical matter our performance is far from this objective. Missionary executive Dr. Clarence Jones observes that "the dollars lost through poor judgment would finance all new projects on the horizon."

Clark Breeding, partner in the nationwide accounting firm of Peat, Marwick and Mitchell, has concluded, "Nothing is so badly managed as Christian money."

All of this is not a consequence of intent, but rather of neglect. To elevate our aim, to utilize all of the resources God has given us, to maximize the results of all our efforts in and for His kingdom ought to be our aim. Governor Mark Hatfield perhaps stated this best in "Excellence, the Christian Standard":

> Our first responsibility is to utilize and mobilize the resources, the capacity, the intellect, the drive, the ambitions and all that God has given us, and to use these to the fullest. That comes first in whatever endeavor to which we are committed. If you are a student or professor in an educational institution, your first responsibility is to perform with the highest degree of excellence as a part of that institution.
> In this particular time in history, we have the greatest opportunity as well as the gravest responsibility to live our lives in a committed manner in order to make the greatest possible impact upon our associates, our institutions, upon all men!

Performance-Measuring

Louis Allen defines this activity of management as "the work a manager performs to record and report work in progress and completed." To record means "to make notation of, to set down in writing"; to report is "to convey information."

The emphasis placed by Allen on recording and reporting information will be appreciated by all managers who are aware of the great distortions to which factual information is subjected by these two processes. We realize that in order to be recorded, facts must be observed. Experience has taught us that in the process of observation a great many factors may be involved, including the value systems of the observer, his sensitivity to the particular situation; the keenness of his powers of observation. "Things are seldom what they seem" is the apt phrase epitomizing the fallibility of depending upon the complete authenticity of facts as observed.

The process of reporting facts as observed threatens even further distortion. We have mentioned the experiment of sending a verbal communication through a group from person to person. Not infrequently the end product bears only the most remote resemblance to the initial message. Semantic difficulties alone, involving the different meanings that may be given the same word or phrase, may account for a great variance in content as the result of transmission.

The manager in a missionary organization, for example, who must evaluate information from fields remote from his office, depends upon the accuracy of the observation of facts in a given situation, and then upon their accurate communication or transmission. Proper information must tell us the essential facts and in an understandable way. Furthermore, if communication is more a matter of securing understanding than transmitting facts, then the *meaning* of the facts being recorded and reported becomes important.

There probably are few Christian organizations which have solved the problem of deciding upon and implementing an effective reporting system. From the foregoing discussion, high-lighting as it does the manager's complete dependence upon knowledge and understanding of what is going on, the tragedy of this failure becomes apparent. Lack of certainty that one is being informed effectively of situations concerning which decisions are required of him, can erode the confidence of a director.

A common experience of management consultants in reviewing office procedures is the discovery that the majority of forms and reports required are no longer fulfilling the purpose for which they were intended. "Forms control" is a significant business today as a result of the ease with which the number and complexity of forms proliferate in the average office situation. We are quick to devise a new form to meet a need, but slow, so very slow, to review the old forms to learn which are no longer even being read, let alone utilized. One noted case concerns a consultant who was so busy discovering all of the forms being used in a large company for a multitude of hazy reasons that it took him several months to catalog them by origin, purpose, distribution and utilization. However, by the time he finished this job he discovered that since he had started the cataloging, so many new forms had been created that he faced another month's work to catalog them. When the manager looks for "time wasters" (see chapter 8), forms offer an excellent place to begin the search.

Accurate, concise, relevant and timely reports are essential to effective management. They do not "just happen," however. Careful preparation in terms of discussion, analysis of need, and most effective utilization will return great dividends. Constant review to weed out unnecessary forms and reports will result in great saving of time and effort.

One of the most interesting concepts in reporting is that of "stewardship-reporting" as recommended by Louis Allen. Suggesting that reports should analyze the stewardship of accountable individuals, Allen proposes that reports account for stewardship of facilities, materials and people entrusted to the care of the person reporting. Thus stewardship-reporting measures an individual as manager of his own organization or division. The difficulty of this kind of reporting is seen in the fact that it depends not only upon normal accounting principles but also upon managerial principles.

The need for reporting the trend, rather than presenting an isolated picture of individual accomplishment, is important. This gives the manager the big picture in perspective that is essential to complete understanding.

A word about unnecessarily complicated accounting procedures is in order for those Christian organizations which have succumbed to the temptation to accept what has been presented. Good accountants concern themselves with detail and frequently find themselves in the role of "watching the pennies" for the organization. Occasionally, the language of finance so permeates budget and finance reports that they become virtually meaningless to the managers for whose use they are intended. At this point managers frequently hesitate to admit their lack of understanding or to require that the reports be recast in understandable terms.

Also there is a tendency for such reports to be unnecessarily complicated. To accommodate the need of the manager or executive for fast information and timely reports, special attention should be given to concise summary-reporting which gives essential information in estimated form on relevant matters where corrective action should be considered immediately. Otherwise control is lost and the manager becomes more a spectator than a participant since all of his information is two to six weeks old when he first sees it. Large companies have developed departments specializing in graphing relevant information for quick and easy understanding of the basic essentials and their presentation to top management. The principle here is applicable to most Christian organizations whose operation is affected seriously by the financial picture.

Finally, to be relevant in the most important aspects, reporting ought to be done in terms of planned accomplishment. Thus progress toward organizational objectives is plotted in a visible manner which is subject to corrective and timely action by the manager. Attention thus is focused on the most important single factor in the organization's work—that of whether or not it is accomplishing or moving toward its objective.

We have looked upon "management-measuring" as the recording and reporting of information about the work of the organization either in progress or already completed. Effective communication involves both sending and receiving reports. Such reports ought to relate to planned accomplishments or objectives and keep managers informed of their progress in this regard. Managers and supervisors ought to be held accountable for the stewardship of the resources under their control. Reports must be in understandable language; relate to job requirements; be kept up-to-date to spur timely action; and emphasize managerial needs before accounting needs.

Performance-Evaluating

Must Christians in positions of management falter at the point of evaluating the performance of others? Probably every manager or supervisor in a Christian organization knows something of the tensions that can surround this question. Either the manager may find himself desperately uncomfortable in the task of judging the actions of others, or the employees may find themselves resenting the judgmental character of appraisal made of themselves or their work.

Allen's definition of "performance-evaluating" helps at once by placing the emphasis upon the work rather than the individual. "It is," he says, "the work a manager performs to appraise work in progress and results secured." So we find at once that we are looking at *work* primarily, not at the *person* who performed it. What is being *appraised* (this term seems more acceptable than *judged*) is the performance rather than the individual. What could be more logical and necessary following the setting of standards, which tells us where our actions *ought to be,* and the reporting of results, which tell us where we actually *are?*

Self-appraisal of performance has gained great favor among analysts of managerial behavior. No one is closer to the action appraised than the manager whose work is being appraised. Except for the lack of objectivity, he ought to be in the best position to evaluate his own performance, and certainly to take timely corrective action while the activity continues. Perhaps no other incentive can provide a stronger motivation for excellent performance than availability of appraisal of results.

The principle of "management by exception" enunciated earlier helps to clarify an important concept at this point. If what concerns management is the exceptions to, or variances from, the plan—then appraisal efforts ought to be concentrated at these strategic points. There may be little benefit in appraising what went according to plan, except in certain circumstances where even better alternatives are sought for answers to problems successfully handled previously. Thus we evaluate the variances as a result of which corrective action can be implemented more effectively.

The allowable limits of tolerance in deviating from the plan are an important matter for consideration. In discussing performance with subordinates, managers are cautioned not to overlook deviations within allowable limits, since such tacit acceptance of "allowable deviations" may tend to define new limits of the standards desired. Progressive deterioration of standards would be the almost certain consequence of this oversight.

It has been said that Christian organizations frequently refuse to utilize managerial procedures which are Biblically based, and which secular organizations have used successfully for years. One such procedure is the appraisal interview. As a result of the failure to utilize this proven procedure, many Christian organizations discover too late that basic misunderstandings about responsibilities, authority, assignments and performance have festered beneath the surface and ultimately reaching unmanageable proportions. Regular appraisal offsets this tendency and enables such natural differences to be identified by both supervisor and employee, discussed and corrected.

The greatest benefit received from the appraisal initiated by the person whose work is being appraised is the lessening of tension which otherwise could result. A person asked to evaluate his own work is often more critical than his manager would be. On the other hand, when faced with the prospect of "being told where he was wrong," this same employee will probably become defensive over the very same points. In addition, the objectivity provided by performance standards also tends to diminish potential tension by keeping the focus on the *work* rather than the *person*.

There is an axiom in management that "people have a right to know how they are doing." Managers in Christian organizations ought to go one step further. People *must* know how they are doing. The injustices done to people in the name of "saving them embarrassment" are multiplied over and over again. What greater disservice can be done a person than to hide the facts from him so that he can do nothing about improving his situation? If his talents are not being fully utilized where he is, is it not a service to both him and his Lord to do everything possible to help him either equip himself adequately for this position or to find another where he fits?

But how does a manager do this diplomatically? First he identifies the problem in its incipient stages, before it becomes critical. Then, instead of "pushing it under the rug" in the vain hope that it may disappear, he thinks creatively as he seeks for a way to discuss the problem. No better way has ever been devised than the performance-appraisal system we have been considering. When such a program is applied uniformly across the organization, the personal element is removed and the matter becomes routine. Most important of all, the system aids in the identification of problem areas before they reach the critical and oftentimes uncontrollable stages.

The Presidents' Association of the American Management Association introduced its new A.M.A. handbook, *What to Do About Performance Appraisal*, by Marion Kellogg, with the following observation:

One of the most demanding and continuing responsibilities facing a manager is appraising the performance of his subordinates. It is an essential, day-to-day management activity, for without appraising he cannot promote or fire, counsel or criticize, coach or transfer. Without appraising he cannot truly manage.

Performance-Correcting

"Correcting of performance," says Louis Allen, "is the work a manager performs to regulate and improve methods and results." In the Preface to her excellent work on the subject, *What to Do About Performance Appraisal,* Marion Kellogg urges strong action to achieve this goal: "Let the manager look to the reason for his appraisal and select an instrument designed for his purpose. Having made his appraisal, let him select and carry out a course of action which will resolve his problems or achieve his purpose."

Miss Kellogg's theme is the admonition from *The Mikado,* "Let the punishment fit the crime." While this may cause us to wince a bit, its clarity and decisiveness serve a useful purpose. Much that masquerades as corrective action in Christian organizations does *not* fit the offense or inadequate performance it is intended to correct. Many who manage to get over the hurdle of appraising inadequate performance are bogged down when attempting to decide what to do about it once it has been identified.

In approaching this most difficult managerial activity of performance-correcting, we are reminded by Louis Allen of three conditions that must prevail for the manager to initiate effective corrective action:

1. He must understand and accept his responsibility; he must know what work he is expected to carry out.
2. He must agree to and accept the standards of performance by which he is judged; that is, he must know what results he is expected to accomplish and agree that they are reasonable and necessary.
3. He must have command over his own performance. If he cannot regulate the present operation and make the changes necessary to secure the results he wants without constantly checking with his superiors, he cannot be expected to carry out corrective action.

Because of the emotional overtones that invariably cloud

the area of performance correction, consultants are in agreement that certain cautions must be observed to insure most effective results. The decision to approach the employee directly as a result of an appraisal (assuming it has not been made in co-operation with the employee) should depend, according to Miss Kellogg, on the relationship existing between the employee and his manager and on the probable receptivity of the employee. No problem should exist here if the employee respects the manager's knowledge in the performance area and believes the manager is sincerely interested in helping him do a better job. She cautions, however, that, unfortunately, managers frequently tend to overestimate the soundness of the relationship between employees and themselves. This is true, she continues, not only because their own evaluation of themselves is involved but also because employees often hide resentment, dislike, disparagement and other unfavorable attitudes which might harm their relationship with the boss. In all relationships an employee's perception of the manager's competence and interest in helping him do a better job is a critical factor. Miss Kellogg maintains that the manager is admittedly able to get only an imperfect grasp of this view. Therefore it will always be safer, when one is implementing or coaching appraisal decisions, to assume that a poorer relationship exists than may actually be the case.

Factors affecting employee receptivity which warrant thoughtful review include (1) differences in age and experience; (2) rivalry; (3) unusual work pressures; (4) health; (5) off-the-job pressures; (6) length of time on the job; (7) desire for advancement; (8) recency of salary increase or other recognition; (9) change in managerial attitude; and (10) historical managerial actions.

Where the manager is unsure of the probable receptivity even after considering the foregoing factors, he may elect to experiment with a small suggestion to observe reaction; to ask the employee how he feels about trying a few suggestions for performance improvement; to wait for the employee to ask or suggest that he is ready to discuss performance improvement; to proceed on the basis of past experience, assuming the employee will respond as before, or choosing an indirect approach.

In the appraisal interview itself, self-criticism may be minimized by concentration on the standards for action which were mutually agreed upon initially. The manager should keep the emphasis on the "we" aspect rather than the "you" and upon the "action" or "results" rather than upon the person. When the employee has the opportunity for identification of his own mistakes first, he is in a much more secure position than when he learns his mistakes for the first time from his manager in a direct confrontation situation. Attention should be concentrated on matters that are of significant importance to insure that the effect of the interview is not scattered over too broad and unimportant an area. Maximum participation and communication should be sought at every stage to overcome emotional resistance.

Finally, management should assume the posture of "looking first to itself for the causes of ineffective performance." Improper instruction; inadequate instruction; lack of insuring understanding of assignment; poor communication—these are a few of the causes which can be corrected by the manager himself and they are appropriate areas of discussion with the employee. Allen concludes as follows:

> When taking corrective action, every variance should prompt a check to ensure that the cause of the exception is not an inadequacy of our underlying management. In this way, we can use our controls to ensure that we are accomplishing the results we want, within the limits we have set for ourselves. This is the final test of professional management.

CHAPTER 13

TIME ROBBERS

Are you on top of your job or underneath it? Many men in the high-pressure world of business and industry look on helplessly while their responsibilities grow faster than they can handle them.

—Auren Uris

INEFFICIENCY may rank first among all time robbers. A job done poorly, whether in haste or carelessness, that must be done over, is a monstrous thief of time. Expand the category of work poorly done to include work not completed, necessitating retracing of footsteps (such as the review of a record without drawing conclusions ... requiring restudy of the same material), and the magnitude of this problem becomes more apparent.

Inefficiency seems at times to gain a foothold in Christian organizations more easily than in secular organizations. Some observers suggest that the reason for this may be the tendency to overspiritualize problems (to blame them on God instead of facing them and trying to solve them). Others suggest that to apply secular standards of efficiency involves judgment of performance—which causes problems for those who believe that no judgment of another is ever justified where Christians are involved. Still others feel that often the fellowship of Christians is emphasized in such a way as to make efficiency appear to be in conflict with fellowship. Distorted views of organizational structure sometimes result from this emphasis to the point where any organizational hierarchy or authority is resisted. The Scriptural basis of authority was reviewed earlier. Suffice it to say at this point that an organization in which everyone expects literally to take his orders only from God is inviting chaos, confusion and ineffectiveness.

Indecision ranks high among the time robbers. Frequently resulting from the fear of failure discussed in the last chapter, failure to make timely decisions can result in significant long-run waste of effort and loss of time. It has often been observed that a less desirable decision made in a timely fashion and implemented with discernment may result in far more progress than the best decision which is first delayed, then implemented with hesitancy. The risk of decision-making is inherent in the executive position. Those unwilling to take the risks involved do not belong in this position. Most important, yet perhaps least recognized, is the factor of time allowed for corrective action by a decision made and implemented in a timely way. Even if it is not the best decision, prompt action often provides the added margin of time for correction.

Tension, long recognized as a way of life for the business executive, is now becoming a common subject for conversation when Christian executives meet in management seminars. Pursued with great interest is the positive approach of viewing tension as a potentially constructive force within an organization. Tension arises from differing opinions which should be the basis of progress. If no one within an organization ever questioned a policy or a proposed course of action, progress would be in real jeopardy.

"The high value placed on differences—differences among individuals as well as among groups," says David Ewing, "is one of the most important characteristics of the managerial mind."[1] Ewing insists that the administrator must reject the notion that tension should be avoided if at all possible. He views tranquillity in an organization with alarm, associating it with vulnerable departments and sick enterprises. He finds tension not only acceptable but desirable. While setting limits on the desirable amount and drawing a distinction between tension and chaos, between stress and distress, he seeks to use tension in a positive way for the benefit of his organization. The author identifies six types of tension which have value in the administrative scheme and suggests that one of the marks of the executive is the ability to utilize them in a constructive way for his organization.

Speaking of a special type of tension that can be good,

the American Institute of Management has referred to "the spark of divine discontent which convinces managers that there are always better things to do, better ways of understanding why and how they are done.² According to the Institute one of the distinguishing marks of excellent executives is "an intelligent dissatisfaction with their own results."

Many managers admit to working better under pressure. Tension, understood and utilized, can be a very constructive factor in executive effectiveness. It may become harmful when it exceeds our tolerance for it or represents imagined rather than real dangers.

Successful executives, it would seem, have learned to live with tension. They welcome realistic tension as a healthy incentive to greater concentration of effort and thus find that this supposed foe of executive effectiveness can be turned into a very positive asset.

The manager's environment is filled with surreptitious time robbers which, given the chance, will steal the unsuspecting executive blind. Eric Webster points an accusing finger at them in a discerning article which asks the manager if he is steering the ship, or stoking. "If the captain oscillates between bridge and boiler room," says Webster, "a higher head of steam won't compensate for steering in circles."³ Just as captains are supposed to set the course, so managers are supposed to manage . . . beginning with their environment.

Surprisingly, many managers make no effort to establish such control. Time and motion studies have been applied to offices as well as to plants with some highly interesting and useful results. The concept of the "functional desk" arose from such studies and has been accepted by many effective executives and management consultants. Utilizing the most accessible locations for the items used most often at one's desk sounds to most of us like a fairly good idea . . . worth thinking about at least. To a time-and-motion man it is an imperative, and his analysis will quickly make believers out of skeptics.

If continuous contact with your top assistant is essential, it makes little sense to locate his office or desk at the corner of the building most remote from your own. Nor does the ultimate filing location of paid invoices belong on the side of the office opposite to the clerk responsible for the filing. Why should your own filing cabinet be against the wall if you need access to it periodically throughout the day? Are the tools you use most often at your desk located most accessibly—the telephone—your dictaphone?

But control of environment must extend far beyond the physical layout of desks and managerial tools. It must include procedures for communication which, if not controlled, may account for greater waste of executive time than any other single factor.

In the clarion call for improved communications, there are those who see a subtle danger for the executive—that of *overcommunication*. Too much communication can be extremely wasteful of time and effort; damaging to morale as well as to executive efficiency. The wise manager will restrain communication that is unnecessary. The grossest violations occur in written reports which ramble and are unnecessarily verbose. Strong incentives should be provided to induce clear, concise and complete reports. *Meetings and conferences* are commonly cited by executives as one of their worst time wasters. The most effective way to restrain this violator is to question the necessity of meeting in the first place. You have seen, perhaps, the cartoon depicting his nibs, the manager, directing his secretary to "call a meeting on the subject of having fewer meetings"!

Should the purpose of the meeting turn out, as it frequently does, to be the sharing of responsibility for *a* decision which the appropriate person prefers not to face alone, the decision-making function ought to be returned immediately to its proper place. When meetings are unavoidable, there are many steps which can lead to limiting unnecessary communication and consequent waste of time. Among such steps are:

(1) Assurance that only those persons necessary for the discussion are present.

(2) Adequate preparation of an agenda and facts to be presented for consideration.

(3) Effective chairing of the meeting to insure keeping discussion to the point and achieving a consensus of that subject.

(4) Assurance that the participants understand major points.

(5) Fixing of responsibility for follow-through on decisions.

Of course, the principal point for consideration in the communications environment is the *telephone* ... friend of millions ... enemy of millions more. What a powerful tool when properly controlled! What a devastating time waster when uncontrolled! Yet where is the manager who has clearly thought through his best procedures for maintaining control of both incoming and outgoing calls?

Looking first at outgoing calls, we find that nearly all advisers recommend grouping them. Get your calls out of the way at one time. The speed with which a dozen calls can be made by a determined and time-conscious executive on his own initiative has amazed more than one manager. Have your facts marshalled so you are prepared to make your own contribution to the conversation expeditiously. In the light of controlling events, remember that every call *you* make to another person is done at a time of *your* own choosing. Calls *others* make to you are done at times of their own choosing. Thus, when you say to a friend or associate, "Give me a call when you're ready," you are inviting an interruption. On the other hand, if you say, "I'll call you in a day or two," you have maintained the initiative and can make the call when you are ready to talk and find it convenient.

Not only should initiative be maintained, but brevity should also be sought. Failure to handle the manager's end of the phone conversation with dispatch was the point of a timely cartoon in the *Wall Street Journal*. The manager looked very imposing and one could hear the imperious quality of his gruff voice:

Hello ... Merrill, Lynch, Pierce, Fenner and Beane? This is Carleton Richardson Henderson III, over at Batten, Barton, Durstine and Osborne.

Hello, are you still there? ...

Hello ... hello. ...

Are you the type of executive who primarily initiates or primarily reacts? Do you wait for situations to develop before considering what action may be required to guide and influence events or do you consider how to initiate events in the first place? Your response to this question, which you may never have asked yourself, may indicate whether the events which surround you tend to control you or whether you tend to control them. We have all observed friends or associates whose jobs have gotten the better of them ... their jobs are running them, we say. It would seem clear that the function of an executive is to do more than simply react. The manager who merely reacts will likely be encircled with problems because events are in control of him. The manager who initiates will probably be involved in opportunities because he is moving in anticipation of events and with the expectation of controlling them instead of letting them control him. Thus the critical question asked by Eric Webster—"Who's in charge?"—applies to the manager and his environment. He will control it . . . or it will control him.

Perhaps the most devastating factor with which to contend in the battle for control over our environment is the *incoming telephone call.* On this tactical battlefield lie the shattered nerves of many a manager who conquered other more imposing time robbers. Executives with secretarial help head inexorably down the road to defeat when they fail to give their secretaries authority in this critical area. If, as some maintain with apparent plausibility, the secretary is not able to handle such responsibility, she should be trained to do so or the responsibility transferred to another. The telephone company has capable training supervisors in charge of customer relations who can handle such an assignment in excellent fashion. The battle of the telephone, from the standpoint of executive control, begins with the first one to lift the receiver.

It is true that the person on the phone represents the organization to the public, and, therefore, courtesy and respect are of paramount importance. But do not forget that of all the surreptitious time wasters surrounding the executive, the telephone is the most successful.

Begin by authorizing your secretary, or the switchboard operator, or an assistant, to screen your calls. Consultants estimate that more than fifty per cent of all calls to executives can be handled—therefore they *ought* to be!—by others. For the assistance of the person doing the screening, list those persons from whom you will always wish to take a call. List circumstances of an emergency nature in which you will always wish to be called. Have a clear understanding of how other calls should be handled —how to request the name of the caller and the purpose of the call; how to refer calls to the appropriate person; how to handle the insistent caller. For those managers who are plagued by merciless telephonic interruptions but lack the courage to end them, perhaps a picture of futility will help:

Visualize a harried manager who finally decides to close his door at times to indicate to his assistant and others that he does not wish to be interrupted. His assistant, an enterprising and determined occupant of a middle-management position, makes the delightful discovery that his boss is always available by phone whenever the door is closed. In fact, he is more approachable than at other times ... seems more relaxed ... and less inclined to end the conversation. Amazing discovery! The assistant wishes he'd close the door more often, since telephoning works so well ... and doesn't take up so much of the assistant's time!

Beyond a doubt, the random ringing of the telephone, uncontrolled, can ruin the best-planned day of any executive.

Incoming mail ... its handling ... and distribution ... poses one of the most surprising of all time wasters. First in order of unforgivable sins, of course, is that committed by the executive who is so anxious to "keep the feel" of the organization that he insists on opening the mail himself. The "feel" of any organization struggling to survive under this level of management ought to be too alarming to "keep."

More often, the inefficiencies connected with incoming-mail-handling occur first in the failure to effect appropriate sorting. At whatever point of distribution is feasible, the executive's mail ought to be classified and the urgent communications, regular communications, and third-class mail separated conveniently. Matters appropriate for handling by assistants or associates ought to be referred immediately, probably with notes to that effect put in their places. A communication which calls for information or data from other departments for proper response ought to have that data noted in the margin with the source noted, if important. Key dates or facts might helpfully be underlined. Facts required but not immediately available should be so noted, with the understanding that the memo or letter will be returned to the executive's desk as soon as the secretary is able to obtain the necessary information. Routine letters or memos should be placed on the executive's desk along with the answers prepared for his signature by the secretary. The principle of delegating authority to the lowest level consistent with good judgment has an extremely important application in the efficient use of a secretary. Excellent use of this principle has been observed in at least one Christian organization where well-trained secretaries are expected to handle up to seventy-five per cent of all correspondence on this basis.[4]

The principle of restraining unnecessary communication has application in the dictation of responses to correspondence. Shorter answers are possible, and therefore desirable, in a great majority of responses dictated by executives. As a check, have your secretary review your letters and memos from a given day or week for a quick estimate of how many of them could have been written in considerably fewer words. Slight effort in this area will yield many minutes in the average day. When you include in time saved that which formerly went into reading unnecessarily long memos from others in your organization, the combined savings of time may be out of all proportion to your expectations.

The place of communications as an element in the executive environment requiring control seems clear. As Reginald Allen, a methods consultant with E. I. du Pont de Nemours, concluded, "A manager must tighten up his communication techniques just as he does production techniques. He must make sure they are getting him closer to his objectives with the least waste of time."[5]

While inefficiency has been listed as a factor in the waste of time, *overconcern or preoccupation with efficiency* may be equally serious. Auren Uris, writing on "The Hazards of Efficiency," cautions the executive against "the emphasis on efficiency without regard to results."[6] This can result in loss of the over-all objective. Such shortsighted misapplication of emphasis is the point of the cartoon depicting the new Ivy League recruit under the watchful eye of his superior. "Blasphington," observes the boss, "I have the impression that you're not very efficient."

"Maybe so," replies the rookie, "but, sir, somebody's got to get the work done around here."

Efficiency that puts method ahead of results may be totally ineffective. We can readily visualize the time wasted *in the long run* by a drive for efficiency which obscures the final objective and necessitates doing the job over. Perhaps this was the observation leading to the slogan now seen occasionally in work areas:

> If you don't have time to do it right,
> When will you have time to do it over?

No list of time wasters would be complete without including the *casual visitor*. No executive is immune to this phenomenon ... unless perchance he works behind security barriers in classified governmental operations. And even there the casual drop-in visitor may be the manager in the office next door. What is your philosophy about such interruptions? Would you, like many other executives, frown at the suggestion of extending a ten-minute coffee break by ten extra minutes to complete a meaningful visit ... but welcome the intrusion of an unannounced visitor from another department who "passes the time of day" not for ten minutes, but, let us say, half an hour?

Consider, for a moment, the matter of justice and equity with respect to those who need time with you. When a drop-in visitor comes unannounced and without having made an effort to arrange an appointment, and you give him as much time as he chooses to take ... what are you doing to the rights of others who are expected to make appointments and to respect reasonable time limits?

Next, consider fairness to yourself. If the caller merely wanted to greet you, how much time should this have required? If, in fact, he had a purpose in mind, are you entitled to the respect and courtesy of an appointment so that you can prepare for his visit and give the matter undivided attention?

Finally, consider fairness to the visitor himself. How is he helped by your encouraging this type of unannounced drop-in visit? Many executives have found that a warm, friendly word or two *in the reception area*, not the office, will convey the idea that their schedules have been previously arranged, probably by visitors waiting there in the reception area, who planned ahead. A friendly "Let's plan for time when we can really visit, either here or at lunch" will suffice in most cases. Admittedly, God's will and the providence of circumstances have a place in such considerations. But so also does the orderly and systematic planning essential to effectively carrying out the tasks He has already set before us.

The manager who hasn't thought through how to handle this situation will be at the mercy of his environment and will be fortunate if he accomplishes much if anything of his own choosing during his busiest days.

Twenty-five heads of Christian organizations meeting in Chicago at a management seminar were asked to list the greatest time robbers they faced. The following, not arranged in any particular order, were included in their list:

Misplaced items	Lack of preparation (conferences, etc.)
Visitors (drop-ins)	Correspondence delays (shuffling papers)
Unanticipated interruptions	Reading material not relevant to job
Commuting	Unnecessary correspondence (outgoing)
Long letters	Telephone interruptions
Waiting for people	Poor organization
Failure to delegate	Coffee breaks
Mediocre personnel (instruction required)	Procrastination
	Routine detail

We have said that the problem which is well stated is half solved. So also with respect to time robbers. Their clear and unequivocal identification is a great step in the direction of their control. With some, control will begin almost automatically upon identification. Consider, for example, "lack of preparation for a conference." Once this problem is viewed from the perspective of time wasted—(that time which, because of poor preparation for the conference, had to be spent later in reconvening the group to make the decision they could have made at the first meeting)—the corrective measure will likely be applied automatically to the conference for which you are presently in the process of preparation. When the extent of time wasted by telephone interruptions becomes evident to you from the chart on page 58, you will find yourself and your secretary automatically applying remedial measures to the handling of incoming calls.

Many of the time robbers will require much more control than this, however. Careful analysis of how and why you do the things you do may be necessary in many cases. Procrastination, for one, will likely represent a deeply rooted habit which will not easily surrender. Analysis, a plan of action, and commitment to successful implementation will be required for many. This is why, in the Preface, the reader was cautioned not to read further if he wasn't ready for battle. No, this task plainly is not for the faint of heart. But the rewards for those who persevere far exceed the pain that must precede the victory.

REFERENCES

[1]—Ewing, David W., *The Managerial Mind,* the Free Press, New York, 1964.

[2]—American Institute of Management, *Manual of Excellent Managements.*

[3]—Webster, Eric, "Let's Repeal Parkinson's Law," *A.M.A. Management Review,* December, 1962.

[4]—Far Eastern Gospel Crusade, 14625 Greenfield, Detroit, Michigan.

[5]—Allen, Reginald, "How to Reach Department Goals Faster," *Supervisory Management,* April, 1965.

[6]—Uris, Auren, *The Efficient Executive,* McGraw-Hill, New York, 1957.

CHAPTER 14

MAKE THE TIME YOU NEED

*Show me a way to get more things done. If it works, I'll
pay anything within reason.*

—Charles M. Schwab

WE HAVE TALKED about time robbers ... some brazen, like
the drop-in visitor who expects to take as much of your
time as he feels inclined to ... some surreptitious, who,
like thieves in the night, will never be discovered if not
pursued. Tremendous savings in time have already been
cited as benefits of the identification and handling of time
robbers.

But more rewards lie ahead for the determined manager
who is eager to try all possible routes to the land of
successful time management. Consider *the concept of
"time is money"* developed by specialists on the staff of
Science Research Associates. No executive has any problem realizing that the supply of money in his personal
checking account may have to be subjected to the disci-
pline of a budget if it is to survive the onslaught of
modern-day living. When one views time as money ... of
which a limited supply is available to cover everything
that must be done ... a budget suddenly appears essential
to preserve the time available and to accomplish what
most needs to be done.

Now, few of us can pretend that this is our normal way
of operating. Most of us spend our time as if it were going
out of style. Here a lick ... there a lick ... an odd job or
two ... a few tasks we really looked forward to because
we like doing them ... and perhaps one of the really
important but unpleasant duties that couldn't be avoided

any longer. Our budget of time would look shockingly ragged.

But, say the "time is money" men, consider the problem as if you were operating on a financial budget. You would check the amount available and the amount that would be received during the period ahead.... Then you would review your objectives, determining their priority of importance and urgency. ... Then you would decide on the best application of money to particular projects to accomplish the most in terms of your objectives.

So with respect to *time*. What do you want to get done? ... In what order of importance? ... Over what period of time? ... What is the time available? ... What is the best strategy for application of time to projects for the most effective results? Each of these steps has been discussed in previous chapters. However, pulling them together within a concept similar to financial budgeting has helped many managers not only to see the wisdom of the plan but to implement it with determination.

The staggering amount of material which most executives have to review begins with reports and memos serving as their lifeline to vital organization information ... continues through articles in trade publications, trade association reports, and perhaps books ... and, hopefully, ends with management-development materials to enable them to stay current with evolving managerial principles, methods and techniques. Attention to *increasing their speed and comprehension in reading* would seem imperative, even to the most casual observer. President Kennedy is said to have increased his reading rate from 250 words per minute to more than 1200 per minute. Courses have proliferated and books on management now commonly refer to this important subject. Consider what a modest doubling of your reading speed, with the normal increase of comprehension, could mean to the time-bank account! If the average executive spends three hours a day in reading—letters, memos, reports, at work and at home— we see the possibility of picking up *ninety minutes per day* by an increase in reading speed which, by all standards, would have to be accepted as modest indeed.

For an excellent treatment of this subject, see Carl Heyel's *Organizing Your Job in Management* in which Dr. Hilda Whitener Yoder, of the Yoder Center for Reading Improvement in New York City, presents a speed-reading and comprehension test for the reader along with a number of suggestions.[1] Because of the importance of this factor in executive efficiency and effectiveness, the test and table for interpretation of results is reproduced here with the permission of the American Management Association.

To evaluate your speed, try a little test at this point. The 500-word selection immediately following, between the headings "Starting Time" and "Finishing Time," is of standard difficulty as found in newspapers and general magazines. It largely follows an interview between Heyel and Dr. Yoder and highlights some of the problems of reading speed and comprehension confronting businessmen. Before reading it, note the time you start and then enter your finishing time at the end of the example. Consult the accompanying table to find your reading speed.

Starting Time _____

Chances are good that you are stuffing your brief case with more and more material to read at home. In virtually all middle- and top-level jobs the flood of "required reading" has steadily increased.

Yet most businessmen could cut drastically—or even eliminate—the amount of such work they take home. The secret: developing more efficient reading habits.

Statistics show that most businessmen read below the college level—attaining only three hundred words a minute or less—, that their comprehension of the material is far too low, and that ninety per cent of them could at least double their reading speed and—much more important—boost their comprehension considerably.

To a slow reader, increasing speed and comprehension may seem impossible. He is likely to feel that the ability to read fast is a God-given talent possessed by only a favored few.

Actually, the rapid reader has received no such mystic blessing. The way a person reads is nothing more than a habit. And the slow poor reader, by study and application, can usually become a good reader.

One way to change your reading habits is to go to a good clinic or teacher for a special course. This may well double or even triple the average executive's reading speed. One reason for this is the fact that methods for analyzing reading faults have been developed on a highly scientific plane. Here is just one example. The actual movements of your eye can be photographed, giving a graphic picture of such things as the number of fixations per line of type, backtracking, and length of time required to read a specific number of words.

But can you improve your reading skill on your own, without going to a professional source? Yes—if you are willing to study and practice. Merely reading a book about how to improve your reading won't solve the problem, any more than merely reading about exercise will strengthen your muscles.

Here are the broad principles involved. Authorities have found that most businessmen are likely to be perfectionists in reading. They read every word because they are afraid of missing something. Reading whole thoughts and phrases increases both speed and comprehension.

The best way to do this is by reading material of standard difficulty, such as most popular magazines or light novels. Time yourself and see how much you have read in approximately ten minutes. Next day read for the same length of time but try to read more text.

While doing this, concentrate on moving forward. Don't regress, or look back, trying to pick up something you missed. You will have trouble getting the full meaning at first, but the important thing here is to jostle yourself out of old reading habits.

One way to test your comprehension is to have someone ask you questions on what you have just read. A better way is to do this reading from books specifically designed to improve your skill. They include tests on comprehension that relate to their text.

Finishing Time _____

Minutes	Words per Minute
5	100
4½	110
4	125
3½	143
3	166
2½	200
2	250
1½	333
1	500

To evaluate your comprehension of what you have just read, circle the answers to the following true-false questions about it. Answers are given at the end of this chapter. Give yourself ten points for each correct answer.

(1) To cut his homework, a businessman needs to develop better reading habits.   T   F

(2) Ninety-nine per cent of the businessmen can improve their reading.   T   F

(3) Good reading is a maker of good habits.   T   F

(4) Reading habits can be analyzed.   T   F

(5) Reading techniques can be improved merely by knowing your difficulties.   T   F

(6) Perfectionists who must note every detail tend to be poor readers.   T   F

(7) Reading can be improved by looking for whole thoughts and phrases.   T   F

(8) The best way to improve reading is to choose for daily practice a book you find difficult to read.   T   F

(9) Looking back for a missed idea is a "must."   T   F

(10) Comprehension can be developed by reading books written for this purpose.   T   F

Score (Per Cent)	Rating
60 or Lower	Poor
70	Passing
80	Good
90	Very Good
100	Excellent

This preview of the problem of slow reading and the view of the reader's own speed and comprehension of reading should provoke further action. If a reputable course is not available in a near-by college or university or professional center, Heyel's book will offer an excellent beginning.

The "overworked" executive who stays late and lugs home a bulging brief case has doubtless read the old adage "Don't stay late . . . delegate." Despite the fact that much has been written about this critical management tool, it still may be the least utilized of all the powerful aids at the command of the modern executive. We assume, of course, that the manager has assistants so that delegation is feasible as a solution to his problem of overwork. The chances are that for many reasons—(some relating to him, others to his subordinates)—the full benefits to be gained from effective delegation are not being realized. While delegation has been treated in greater detail in Chapter 8 in a discussion of "What Managers Do," its place among the foremost timesavers requires mention here. Most managers, when they face the ultimate question regarding delegation—"What am I doing that ought to be done by one of my associates?"—come up with a surprising list. If none of the other well-known reasons for delegating come to mind, let's hope that the manager at this point at least considers the experience and opportunities for learning of which he is depriving his subordinates.

Do It to a Finish was a book written in 1909 by Orison Marden concerning the tragedy of the carelessness and blunders of those who never formed the habit of accuracy, thoroughness and of doing things to a finish.[2] A lament to the uncompleted task, and the philosophy of life which spawns it, this fascinating work calls "a blessing to civilization" men who can do things to a finish, who complete what they undertake, who leave nothing half done. "Make it a life-rule," the author pleads, "to give your best to whatever passes through your hands. Stamp it with your manhood. Let superiority be your trade-mark; let it characterize everything you touch."

Although the words may be slightly different, author Marden's philosophy so well articulated at the turn of the century applies with great force to the criteria of management today. James Menzies Black lists *stamina* (persistence, staying power) third among his "Qualities of Executorship."[3] The "doctrine of completed work," according to Louis Allen, holds that the manager who can delegate to the men under him the responsibility to do a "whole job" is helping himself as well as his organization. A Christian businessman, who has served on a number of boards of Christian organizations, makes certain that his subordinates in business know they are expected to bring answers, not problems. If problems are brought, it is understood that this is because they have tried without success to find answers.

Executive search firms, in reviewing candidate qualifications for top executive positions, take particular interest in what a man's record says about projects initiated and carried out. "How is he on follow-through?" is a critical question. It relates not only to the probability that the man can be depended upon to conclude a project, but more importantly, also to the certainty that *the time already invested in the project has not been wasted.*

The twenty-five Christian executives whose list of "greatest time robbers" appeared in the last chapter were also asked to list their "greatest time-savers." Among the items arousing most interest were the following:

The Committee of Two—Avoid involving any unnecessary persons in the decision-making process.

Correspondence—fast answers. Scribble response on letter or memo. Xerox copy for your file. Return original.

Correspondence—Handle only once—Don't put it back in the pile! Answer it or get it where it can be answered.

Correspondence follow-up file—If you must wait for information before answering, mark for F/U file (i.e., one week). Secretary pulls out in one week and returns to you with information necessary for answer.

Insure understanding when delegating—Extra time invested to insure complete understanding pays big dividends in time saved ultimately!

Appointments by secretary—Time taken to develop good system of handling appointments pays off.

Delegate reading—Why not? Benefits others besides yourself. Also gives you picture of other talents of your team, while enormously broadening your coverage of important materials.

Conference phone call with pre-arranged agenda—Can accomplish amazing results at a fraction of cost in time and travel money. From three to perhaps six persons in as many cities on the same hookup.

Have secretary answer correspondence—Aim to delegate as much of the correspondence as she can handle well. One organization aims for seventy-five per cent to eighty per cent of all correspondence by secretaries, who sign the boss's name and present complete file to him with letter for signature.

Shorter memos and letters—Conscious effort here can bring amazing results.

Wastebasketry—Master the "quick toss" technique!

Form letters—Where personal touch is not essential.

Planning and organizing time—A look ahead may be worth two behind!

A good secretary—Worth her weight in gold! Excellent seminars offered for executive secretaries.[3]

Management training—Careful selection of an occasional seminar provides needed break . . . objective view . . . solutions others have found to same problems . . . current thinking in profession of management.

Trained staff—All of foregoing applies to staff . . . set example . . . expect them to follow (let them know your expectations) . . . follow-up.

The list could go on . . . endlessly perhaps? Many suggestions have almost universal application. That is why management has developed so rapidly into a profession. But many of the timesavers will be personally oriented to the manager's own style and technique. Whatever works best for you . . . wherever you find your timesavers . . . never forget that the success or ultimate effectiveness of managers depends primarily upon *how they use their time*.

Answers to questions on page 191

1 – T	6 – T
2 – F	7 – T
3 – T	8 – F
4 – T	9 – F
5 – F	10 – T

REFERENCES

[1]—Heyel, Carl, *Organizing Your Job in Management*, American Management Association, New York, 1960.

[2]—Marden, Orison Swett, *Do It to a Finish*, Thomas Y. Crowell and Company, New York, 1909.

[3]—Black, James Menzies, *Assignment: Management*, Prentice-Hall, Inc., New Jersey, 1961.

CHAPTER 15

ARE YOUR "PROBLEMS" REALLY "OPPORTUNITIES"?

When all kinds of trials and temptations crowd into your lives, my brothers, don't resent them as intruders, but welcome them as friends!

—James 1:2 (Phillips Translation)

THROUGHOUT this book has been woven a thread which must not be overlooked. Perhaps it is a thread of opportunity . . . perhaps of realism . . . in any event, of hope. It lies in the suggestion that many of our apparent problems, including the most enervating, could be opportunities in disguise. We mentioned, for example, that sometimes we ought *not* do today what can be put off till tomorrow. In deliberate delay we may find an answer to the "tyranny of the urgent." These matters which have a way of pressing in relentlessly seem more important than they really are. Urgent? Perhaps. Vitally important? Probably not. Turning now to a brief consideration of a few of the more grievous problems faced by Christian executives, we will attempt to determine whether they may be opportunities in disguise.

Failure . . . Your Greatest Fear, or Best Teacher?

Of all the problems facing the executive, fear of failure almost always places at or near the top. The higher one rises on the ladder of responsibility, the greater seems to be the premium placed upon success, and, conversely, the greater the risk of failure. This seems logical when one considers the enlarging scope of decisions, the widening range of responsibilities. Fear of failure may play a very significant role in the insecurities sensed by an executive just promoted to a more responsible position. Confident and secure in his former position, the man in his new job may suddenly lose the inner sense of well-being which comes only with confidence that he is in the right job and can handle it well. The fact that he performed his former duties may well lead his superiors into a false sense of security about the new assignment. Completely overlooked may be the fact that this is a new job, with entirely new responsibilities, in entirely new surroundings, under entirely different circumstances, with an entirely new team of associates.

Perhaps the greatest tragedy is that the premium placed upon success by our society gives even the man who senses the danger beforehand little chance to say "No."

But how does the man at the top treat failure? What is his attitude toward his own fears in this regard? How does he view the failure of his subordinates?

We know instinctively that the well-adjusted executive who is at home in his job has a more relaxed attitude toward failure. His security permits this. Insecurity breeds uneasiness about the risks involved in critical decision-making. Yet the more insecure one feels about his position and his ability to carry out his responsibilities, the less likely he is to make sound decisions.

Thus the fear of failure must be faced head-on. It is helpful to begin by reminding ourselves that the best managers expect to fail at many points along the way. They will tell you, "Show me a man who hasn't made a mistake and I'll show you a man who hasn't tried anything," for we don't learn anything without trying. And without trying we shall make little progress. More important than the number of mistakes we make as executives are the types of mistakes we make (are they well calculated to be instructive? are they delimited to prevent catastrophic loss?). And let us remember which of our own experiences in life have taught us the most. Our successes? Hardly. Our failures? Most assuredly!

Then why must we fear failure when it has been our best teacher? We must expect to fail . . . but fail in a learning posture, determined not to repeat the mistakes, and to maximize the benefits from what is learned in the process. Many leaders expect to make mistakes steadily but also expect their right decisions to outweigh their wrong ones. Some say that if an executive is right fifty-five per cent of the time, and it's the right fifty-five per cent, success of his organization is assured.

And what about your subordinates? When you delegate a job do you also delgate "the right to be wrong"? Do you tell your employees, and do you mean it, that you expect them to make mistakes? An organization that is not making mistakes is either not trying to accomplish much or is dead. What counts is what you do with your mistakes. You can become their prisoner . . . or use them for stepping-stones.

One management consultant felt so strongly about this factor in the health of organizations that he coined the phrase "Failsmanship." Another called it "Failing forward." Not to know what you believe about this will encourage insecurity in yourself and in those about you. It will stifle creativity, independent thinking and risk-taking.

Incorporated in your philosophy of management ought to be a philosophy of failure. How you view it and how you use it can have a tremendous effect upon your own success, the success of those about you, and the ultimate achievement of your organizational objectives.

Tension . . . Cause for Despair, or Requisite for Progress?

Perhaps the best picture of tension at the top was captured by Auren Uris in his account concerning the executive who walked into the office and sat down at the desk across from the psychiatrist.[1]

> "What seems to be the trouble?" asked the doctor.
> "It's hard to say. I feel under a constant strain. I have trouble sleeping nights. Even when I go away for vacations, I find I can't unwind enough to feel really comfortable."
> "Do I understand that you work for the XYZ Company?"
> "That's right."
> "Then what you tell me is of particular interest. The company has a fine reputation; it is run by an enlightened management. I understand they have a great awareness of the emotional needs of their executives; they do everything possible to make it a good place to work. Have you discussed your problems with the president?"
> "I am the president . . . ."

The adverse effects of tension were discussed in the chapter on "Time Robbers." Also considered was the positive view of tension as a contributive force to the success of organizations. Discerning managers are viewing tension as indicators of health within the organization. Individually, participants in athletic, forensic and other events have long known that tension, to a certain degree, is essential to top performance. We also recognize the familiar executive refrain, "I work best under pressure."

What few managers have discerned is that there are forms of tension which can be a great help individually and organizationally if they are identified and harnessed as constructive forces. Tension, not harnessed, can easily degenerate into conflict which is much less easily managed, and can turn from a potentially constructive force to one of destruction.

As Christians we are not promised freedom from trial and tribulation. We are, however, admonished to welcome them as being sent to test our faith. As Dr. Donald F. Tweedie observes, "Christ alone, the Alpha and Omega, can truly transcend the temporal order and provide the remedy for the guilt of the past and the reassurance for the anxiety of the future.[2]

Differences . . . Prelude to Conflict, or Dynamic Growth?

Conflict resolution is rapidly assuming a major role in management conferences. While much in the field remains to be discovered, it is possible to suggest certain conclusions at this time.

Conflict generally appears to result from differences which had they been identified and dealt with opportunely, would have been much more easily resolved. At the conflict level, required solutions tend to be more drastic, such as termination of the offending person at worst and severe loss of face at best. While the merits of the case and the individual circumstances must determine the approach, speed and directness of approach are almost universally recommended. Getting the facts on the table in a careful and fair way is essential. Where gross inequity exists in the relative merits of the opposing sides, the focus of attention on the real facts sometimes tends to resolve the conflict since the solution tends to suggest itself.

But this is remedial action, not preventive. Much better would be the management of differences *before* they degenerate into conflict. A positive approach to differences was demonstrated by McGeorge Bundy shortly after he left the White House to assume his position as president of the Ford Foundation. In an appearance before the Senate Foreign Relations Committee he was asked about the impact of the DeGaulle visit to Moscow on the Atlantic Alliance and NATO. Bundy responded:

> This is a good time for a careful review of the Atlantic society, but it is not a good time for any hasty judgment that the time has come to put an end to NATO, or even to General DeGaulle. It is certainly not a time for Americans to choose up sides in a sham battle over false issues. *What unites the Atlantic Alliance is still much greater than what divides it.*[3]

Suppose that, at their inception, all differences were first viewed in the light of how they compared with similarities and factors of cohesion! Known to exist in a given situation!

Suppose, too, that differences were encouraged as a sign of the vital and dynamic health of an organization. Creative thought almost inevitably leads to differences. We want and need creative thinking. Hence we ought to encourage the type of differences that spring from such independent thinking. In such an environment, the executive of a Christian organization might well approach a known difference between two of his key department heads in a most constructive way. Suppose that instead of asking one employee about the truth of his statement concerning the ideas of the other, and doing this in the presence of both—an approach in which defensiveness would be the almost certain result—he first thanked them for generating and defending their opposing views. Then suppose that after explaining why he valued differences of opinion highly as signs of a dynamic and vital organization, he complimented them on the independence of thought evidenced by their views. Finally suppose that he asked them to help him select from each position, as they carefully reviewed them, the portions which would best advance the interests of the organizations as a whole toward its objectives.

Will Erickson, in his management seminars entitled "Understanding Differences Among People" and "Handling People's Problems," suggests several steps in a constructive approach to such situations.[4] First he identifies the performance gap which exists between what a person *can* do, dependent upon his physical capabilities, and what he *will* do, dependent upon his attitude, motivation and emotional maturity. The narrowing of this performance gap is a prime objective of the manager. To do this it is essential to take a serious approach to the handling of people's problems and dissatisfactions. While we wish to eliminate as much friction as possible, Erickson reminds us that as long as people are people, we will have some dissatisfactions. Most problems of employees reduce themselves at some point to a matter of communication. Once a problem is known to exist, he recommends fast action to identify it and its causes. Listening is important. The problem should be summarized in the person's own words to insure his agreement that your version of the problem is correct. All essential details should be checked, additional facts obtained and authenticity established. Where relevant, other person's observations should be reviewed along with the personnel record of the person involved and the written policies. When the decision is reached, discussion with the person should be aimed at encouraging him to draw his own conclusion regarding the total situation. If disciplinary action is necessary, it should be taken immediately. If the organization is in error, this should be admitted and corrective action assured. Buck-passing should be avoided and if the person's problem is not settled to his satisfaction, he should be advised of any recourse he may have.

The subject of "The Christian in an Age of Conflict" occupied the attention of Paul and Mary Bechtel, *Christian Life* book editors, recently.[5] In a favorable review of William Pinson's *How to Deal with Controversial Issues*,[6] the central conviction cited was that Christians can deal with conflict constructively and redemptively. "The character of the Christian as set forth in the New Testament," observes Pinson, "is ideal for dealing with controversial issues." The Christian life, add the reviewers, cultivates love, kindness, unselfishness, humility, courage, wisdom, lack of prejudice—all strong assets with which to confront conflict. Yet most local churches shun controversy by ignoring, repressing, or glossing over it. The author's work is recommended as a manual of principles of common-sense suggestions for the orderly approach to controversial issues. Many conflicts of opinion grow in bitterness and find no resolution because the groundwork for discussion has never been properly charted.

One authority on the subject of conflict describes its relation to power:

> It follows that the more prevalent conflict in an organization becomes, the more keenly will the need for power be felt and the more ardently will it be sought. This is true because power is by definition the ability to induce change in the behavior of others, and, the more disagreement and conflict which exist between the wishes of each actor and the behavior of others, the greater is the motivation of each to find ways of changing the others. Out of the need to induce such changes, each member of the organization becomes a seeker of power and, if the search is successful, a wielder of power.[7]

Perhaps the desirability of disagreement or differences of opinion within organizations, within limits, was best summarized by Sydney J. Harris, well-known syndicated columnist, who observed:

> The commonest way to cheat an employer is not by stealing his money or loafing on the job, but by refusing to disagree when you feel he is wrong. If he is paying you for your brains, you have an obligation to dissent from decisions you think wrong.[8]

Differences of opinion may indeed be a prelude to conflict or, with discerning management, become a primary ingredient in the growth of a vital, dynamic organization.

Loneliness . . . to Be Pitied, or Sought After?

As every top manager knows, the chief executive of an organization holds "the loneliest job in the world." If his rise to the top has been through the ranks of his own organization, the gradual erosion of fraternal ties may have been painfully evident to him and leave him even more sensitive to the isolation at the top. We have no one with whom to share our gravest problems, say many such top executives. Some seek out others with similar responsibilities so that they can exchange ideas and share problems and solutions. Christian management seminars have sprung up from this single primary motivation. When the executive identified by Auren Uris earlier in this chapter was asked if he had discussed his problems with the president, his response, "I am the president," spoke graphically of this world of solitude.

But wait. What could be better for the harried, over-burdened executive? The manager described at the outset in the Preface must have yearned for escape from the stacked desk to which he felt enslaved, from the crushing pressure of crises, from the tyranny of time. *Ah, for just an hour of peace and solitude,* he must have sighed, recognizing his need for reflection and contemplation. Thus the loneliness that one executive finds oppressive becomes the oasis of another.

The price of leadership is high. Among its most exacting tolls is the position described by authors in the field as that of the "isolate." Yet, viewed in its most constructive light, this penalty or price of leadership can also be its most redeeming feature. If the chief executive should be spending from one-third to one-half of his time planning ahead, how better can this be done than by taking advantage of the relative isolation at the top? The most successful executives go to great lengths to set aside and preserve such time, safeguarded from interruption and the demands of the routine. Louis Evans, Jr., has described the tremendous value of a day of solitude, away from phones, associates and family, in helping him to prepare his weekly sermon. Thus once again a serious problem is seen at second glance as a great opportunity.

Problems . . . End of Leadership or the Beginning?

The list of such problems could be extended to demonstrate that within each lie the seeds of opportunities awaiting nurture and development by the discerning manager. Are we saying then that much of the managerial environment consists in how we view it? Are we saying that situations which some consider to be oppressive handicaps appear to others to be exciting opportunities? Are we saying that, upon reflection, you may find yourself surrounded with resources for improving your managerial performance? So it would seem.

> Two men looked out the selfsame bars
> One saw mud . . . the other, stars.

When problems pile up around a leader and solutions seem unavailable, it is logical that he begin to question his own leadership. "Perhaps," he may say, "it is time for new leadership. After all, shouldn't a leader have answers?"

In the age of the "generalist" the answer to this question appears to be negative. As the job of the executive becomes more complex, it is less and less possible to be technically competent in all fields (computerization and motivation of personnel, to name but two of many). Thus for the man at the top it becomes far more important to know the right questions than to worry about the right answers. Of course he must recognize answers when they appear. But to be able to ask intelligent, discerning questions may be the critical managerial skill at this point. These questions, as described by an associate who heads an international Christian organization, should elicit critical information concerning objectives, opportunities, resources, and, finally, the strategy for applying maximum resources to the greatest opportunities for the ultimate achievement of objectives.

Thus with James, in his greetings to the twelve dispersed tribes, we may say:

> When all kinds of trial and temptations crowd into your lives, my brothers, don't resent them as intruders, but welcome them as friends! Realize that they come to test your faith and to produce in you the quality of endurance (James 1:2-3, Phillips).

What better way of life, as Tournier suggests, to become exciting adventure!

REFERENCES

[1]—*Op. cit.*
[2]—Tweedie, Donald F., "Faith and Your Feelings: Anxiety," *Eternity*, December, 1964.
[3]—Associated Press Dispatch, *Chicago Sun-Times*, June, 1966.
[4]—President, Will Erickson Associates, Blue Island, Illinois.
[5]—Bechtel, Paul, and Mary, "The Christian in an Age of Conflict," *Christian Life*, April, 1966.
[6]—Pinson, William M., *How to Deal with Controversial Issues*, Broadman.
[7]—Kahn, Robert L., *Power and Conflict in Organizations*, Survey Research Center, University of Michigan.
[8]—Harris, Sydney J., in the *Chicago Daily News*, *Management Review*, American Management Association, April, 1966.

CHAPTER 16

CALL TO EXCELLENCE

If the resources of the country are to be well used, executives and professionals must become, to a greater degree, masters of their own time. Time is a limited and valuable resource that must be allocated among competing objectives—natural, institutional and personal. The needs of each organization and the well-being and development of key personnel, can be advanced or retarded significantly, depending on how well time is planned and used.

—Paul J. Gordon

PROBLEMS or opportunities . . . it's all in how you view them! Looking back we see that many problems have been dealt with which are faced daily by managers. We have also seen the possibility of becoming too "problem-oriented." Opportunities seem to pass by those who are buried in their problems. Another way of looking at this is that problems may *be* opportunities, depending upon our perspective.

First of all, if it weren't for a few problems, why would managers like you be needed? So *problems* do provide an opportunity for management, don't they? *Failure* is both the manager's greatest fear . . . and his best teacher. Where are you going to place your emphasis? *Tension* has been viewed as an ulcer-builder and as a tonic for progress. Will you turn it into a constructive asset? *Decision-making* has been seen as the ultimate risk, but also as the pivotal management skill. Will you abdicate on the quicksand of indecision or welcome this golden opportunity to share in shaping the course of future events? *Disagreement* has within it the seeds of destructive conflict or dynamic growth and vitality. Will you cover it up . . . pretend it doesn't exist . . . hope it will go away—or welcome it immediately as a positive force and manage it into a contributive element in your organization?

Efficiency has been presented as the Christian imperative of responsible stewardship, but distorted at times into a threat to fellowship. Will you permit this contortion of two basic principles or insist upon their separate contributions to life, vitality and purposefulness within your organization? *Loneliness* has been portrayed as the characteristic of top management. Will you pity yourself for having no one with whom to share your deepest problems? Or will you see yourself as a partner with Christ and with His body—your fellowmen ... and, view the solitude of ultimate decisions as an opportunity for contemplation of His divine purpose for your organization and for you? We have viewed *objectives* and their *priority* as something overlooked till now, but imperative for managerial effectiveness.

In Part One *"A Perspective on Work and Time"* was proposed that called for an answer to the question why we work; viewed use of time as a matter of responsible stewardship; and led to the conclusion that the problem isn't time, but ourselves. In Part Two we talked about *"Managing Ourselves"*—since management of time ultimately got down to that. We took inventory of our personal resources (God-given talents); our opportunities implicit in our jobs; and our time (to determine what we were *actually* accomplishing in terms of results with our time). We selected a strategy for matching our resources with our opportunities for maximum results; assessed the time-robbers stealing our most precious asset; learned how others "make the time they need"; discussed managerial self-development; answered the question of why executives choose to work long hours; and reflected on a philosophy of leisure.

In Part Three we reviewed the *"Management of Others."* After a look at the Biblical basis of authority we reviewed philosophies, definitions and principles of management. We then saw *what managers do* when they are managing: planning, organizing, leading, and controlling.

Since management of time is basically a question of *how* we do *what* we do, *all* of the time—we see that wasted effort is wasted time. So what we do and how we do it are ultimate questions in our inquiry. Your answer to these questions will determine the responsibility of your stewardship.

Governor Mark Hatfield summed it up when he said:

Our first responsibility is to utilize and mobilize the resources, the capacity, the intellect, the drive, the ambitions and all that God has given us, and to use them to the fullest. That comes first in whatever endeavor to which we are committed. If you are a student or professor in an educational institution, your first responsibility is to perform with the highest degree of excellence as a part of that institution. In this particular time in history, we have the greatest opportunity as well as the gravest responsibility to live our lives in a committed manner in order to make the greatest possible impact upon our associates, our institutions, upon all men![1]

If we are committed to live for Him the life that He gave to us, we will conclude that in all we do with our time as managers nothing less than the best is good enough. Since our entire life-time is a gift from God, let us manage it for Him!

REFERENCES

[1]—Hatfield, Mark, "Excellence: The Christian Standard," *Collegiate Challenge* Magazine, May, 1965.

FOR YOUR READING PLEASURE

EXTRAORDINARY LIVING FOR ORDINARY MEN by Sam Shoemaker
One of America's outstanding churchmen shows how you can lead an extraordinary life—with the faith that turns the commonplace into an exalted reflection of God.
No. 10778p

HOW TO WIN OVER WORRY by John Edmund Haggai
A practical formula for successful living. Shows how to increase your income, handle criticism, improve your health, deal effectively with people, have peace in the midst of trouble.
No. 9740p

THE ART OF UNDERSTANDING YOURSELF by Cecil Osborne
A powerfully written self-help book that combines psychology and religion as an aid for richer and happier living.
No. 10472p

MANAGING YOUR TIME by Ted W. Engstrom and Alex Mackenzie
Practical suggestions to make the most of yourself . . . and your day. As valuable as an extra hour in the day for the housewife, businessman, student.
No. 9572p

DOES ANYONE HERE KNOW GOD? by Gladys Hunt
Dynamic true stories of 17 women whose lives changed after encountering God and His love, among them: Eleanor Searle Whitney, Jane Stuart Smith, Yoshiko Taguchi, Betty Carlson.
No. 9880p

A TREASURY OF HUMOR by Clyde Murdock
An uproarious collection of more than 500 jokes, puns, anecdotes and humorous stories . . . for all occasions. Conveniently categorized, the subjects are arranged alphabetically for ease of use.
No. 10368p

ENCYCLOPEDIA OF GAMES by Doris Anderson
Choice collection of 686 games in wholesome fun . . . for all occasions and every season . . . many never in print before . . . a boon for youth group leaders and every parent.
No. 9076p

HOW TO MAKE A HABIT OF SUCCEEDING by Mack R. Douglas
Practical guide to harnessing the power of purpose and the might of motivation to produce dynamic action . . . by a man who has applied and improved upon Dale Carnegie's methods.
No. 9536p

THE GOSPEL BLIMP by Joseph Bayly
Reach and inspire with faith one billion people?—with a blimp??? They tried . . . the result: a searching, moving hilarious parable of Christian purpose gone astray . . . a modern masterpiece now in its 5th big printing.
No. 12288p

PRAYER: CONVERSING WITH GOD by Rosalind Rinker
A dynamic explanation of conversational prayer, the spiritual strength it brings and the inner rewards of awaiting His reply . . . 17 printings to date in hardcover . . . "the best, direct, understandable book on prayer"—Baptist Sunday School Board.
No. 10716p

DARE TO LIVE NOW! by Bruce Larson
Shows how life can be changed now for anyone who knows how to appropriate the power and love of God through Christ and presents concretely the how of faith—how to lay hold of God's willingness to help, to heal and to guide in everyday life situations.
No. 10001p